Fearless Female Journalists

The Women's Hall of Fame Series

Fearless FEMALE Journalists

Joy Crysdale

Second Story Press

Library and Archives Canada Cataloguing in Publication

Crysdale, Joy, 1952-
Fearless female journalists / Joy Crysdale.

(The women's hall of fame series)
ISBN 978-1-897187-71-5

1. Women journalists—Biography—Juvenile literature.
I. Title. II. Series: Women's hall of fame series

PN4820.C79 2010   070.92'2   C2010-900610-0

Editor: Debbie Rogosin
Copyeditor: Karen Helm
Designer: Melissa Kaita
Cover photos and icons © istockphoto.com

Printed and bound in Canada

*Second Story Press gratefully acknowledges the support of the Ontario Arts
Council and the Canada Council for the Arts for our publishing program.
We acknowledge the financial support of the Government of Canada through the
Book Publishing Industry Development Program.*

ONTARIO ARTS COUNCIL
CONSEIL DES ARTS DE L'ONTARIO

Canada Council   Conseil des Arts
for the Arts   du Canada

Published by
Second Story Press
20 Maud Street, Suite 401
Toronto, ON
M5V 2M5
www.secondstorypress.ca

*For my parents, Minnie and Bryden Crysdale,
with love and gratitude*

CONTENTS

Introduction 1

Mary Ann Shadd Cary 5

Nellie Bly 15

Margaret Bourke-White 25

Doris Anderson 35

Barbara Frum 45

Katie Couric 55

Anna Politkovskaya 65

Pam Oliver 75

Farida Nekzad 85

Thembi Ngubane 95

Glossary 105

Sources & Resources 107

Acknowledgments 115

Photo Credits 117

INTRODUCTION

All of us want to be brave. Few of us think we are. The women in this book are truly courageous. That doesn't mean they didn't feel fear, or anxiety, or darkness. It means they went ahead anyway and did what they believed they had to do. It was their journalism that was fearless, and through it, each of these women changed the world in some way.

Mary Ann Shadd fought the terrible curse of slavery with every fiber of her being. Margaret Bourke-White strode straight into danger to create a photographic record of the tragic things that happened in war. Anna Politkovskaya never stopped speaking out about the evil she saw, and experienced personally. Farida Nekzad is at risk every day because she reports on the terrible plight of women in Afghanistan.

There are many ways in which journalism can have an impact. It can produce wonder. People were completely mesmerized by the fact Nellie Bly traveled around the world – by herself – faster than anyone could have imagined. It can take away shame. Thembi Ngubane did that by telling her own story of AIDS. And let's not forget, everyone needs to laugh once in a while. Barbara Frum was one of the toughest journalists in the business, but she also delighted in bringing funny and absurd stories to her audiences, and they loved her for that. To be a good journalist, you have to be brave enough not to care what people think of you. If you're in the business of telling people the truth, and that is the business journalists are supposed to be in, there are many people who won't like what you say, and will be angry with you for saying it. Sports reporter Pam Oliver has been publicly taken to task for what she's reported, but she speaks for every honorable journalist when she says she's "not in the business of being liked."

Many women in this book also had the courage to make breakthroughs in workplaces that were mostly male, and that restricted what they could do. Doris Anderson, who literally changed a country through her leadership of a magazine, nearly didn't get the job because of prejudice against her as a woman. Katie Couric insisted she be allowed to do the same kind of interviews as her male co-anchor, and broke the mold for female morning show hosts ever after.

Despite the difficulties, and sometimes the dangers, of journalism, one factor overrides everything. It is one of the world's best jobs. All the amazing women in this book absolutely loved what they did, and do. It's exciting, a life of constant learning and public service, and a way to go where others can't. I learned this when I started in radio at the Canadian Broadcasting Corporation. One of my first stories was about the Toronto Zoo, and I went inside an enclosure with a baby gorilla. She sat beside me, placed her hand against mine, and compared the two. I couldn't believe I was lucky enough to be doing that for my job, and that I was being paid for it. Later in my career, working with Barbara Frum at *The Journal*, and then after that on many other kinds of programs, I continued to feel that way.

One of the reasons this book has been written is because many people don't understand the role of journalism. And yet it is crucial to a free society and democracy. Journalists find things out, and tell the public what they find. If people know about things, they can try to do something about them. In Anna Politkovskaya's Russia, when journalists finally had the freedom to tell the public the truth, the government was forced to stop a war. Truthful information for the public is power for the public.

This book begins with a woman who started a newspaper, and ends with a woman who wrote a blog. In between you will meet women who work in magazines, on television and radio. As you read their stories, I hope you will discover what journalists can be, and what they contribute. And I hope you will be as inspired and moved as I have been. Some of the women are tough, a few disagreeable, and others you might not necessarily want as friends. They were, and are, human, after all. But they are all admirable, and I believe deserve our gratitude for taking on the challenges they did.

There are so many more like them, through history and today, who work hard just to bring us the truth. My only regret about this book is that I couldn't include all the brave women journalists who deserve recognition. We need them. I hope you enjoy meeting these women. And I hope they inspire you to make your own way in the world with courage.

Joy Crysdale

MARY ANN SHADD CARY

"My destiny is that of my people."

1823 - 1893

Mary Ann Shadd didn't care if she made people angry. As a matter of fact, she seemed to enjoy it. If people were going to get in her way when she was doing what she believed to be right, they had better watch out. As one black historian who knew her wrote, trying to stop Mary Ann was as useless as attempting "to remove a stone wall with your little finger." She was a formidable foe, willing to take on anyone in her battles for equality for black people, and for women. Journalism and the written word were Mary Ann's weapons of choice, and they established her place in history. She became the first black woman editor in North America, and some say she was also the first African-American woman to establish and publish

Free Blacks Before 1861

Before the American Civil War, about ten per cent of the black population were not slaves but "free" – although there were many barriers to what they could do. There were a variety of reasons they, or their ancestors, were free; some slaves were released by their owners, some ran away, and some were rewarded with freedom when they fought with the American side in the revolution. Others were freed when some northern states abolished slavery.

a newspaper in Canada or the United States.

Mary Ann was the first of Abraham and Harriet Shadd's thirteen children. She was born in 1823, in Delaware, at a time when slavery was still legal in most of the United States. This cruel practice of people owning other people as pieces of property had been in place since the 1600s, when Africans were forcibly shipped to America to be sold. The Shadds were not slaves; they were part of a small minority of "free" blacks, and their family had been free for generations.

But Abraham and Harriet did not take this good fortune for granted. They were abolitionists: people determined to bring slavery to an end. Sometimes this meant taking risks for themselves and their children. It's believed they helped slaves trying to escape to freedom by making their home part of the Underground Railroad. Anyone caught helping these runaway slaves could be severely punished. The Underground Railroad was not actually a railway at all. "Underground" meant it was secret, and "Railroad" meant it was a way of moving people from one safe place to the next, to destinations where they could be free.

Abraham was a shoemaker, but he also worked as a salesman for *The Liberator* newspaper, which was run by a white abolitionist named William Lloyd Garrison. In the *Liberator's* first issue, published in 1831, Garrison wrote that he would never give up his fight to stop the slave trade. "I will not retreat a single inch – AND I WILL BE HEARD." This newspaper was practicing what is called advocacy journalism: taking a stand on an important moral issue, and advocating for change. Mary Ann grew up with it as a model of how journalism could be used.

By the time Mary Ann was ten, the Shadd family had moved to Pennsylvania, where abolitionists were very active. The Shadds believed education was an important tool for achieving equality, and Mary Ann is said to have been taught by Quakers, a Christian group opposed to slavery. She became a teacher herself at age sixteen, work she continued throughout her life.

One story passed down about Mary Ann as a young woman shows just how determined she was to defy society's rules. She was standing on a street in New York City in the 1850s, needing to get somewhere. Black people weren't supposed to ride on public streetcars, but when one came along, Mary Ann "threw up her head, gave one look, and a wave of her hand." The driver, a very unpleasant man known to refuse rides to black people, was so surprised by her commanding signal that he pulled over. Mary Ann got on and rode to her stop without a problem.

Mary Ann was twenty-five when she started on the path that would establish her place in journalistic history. It was 1849, and the *North Star*, another abolitionist newspaper, asked readers to write in with their solutions to the problems of poverty and discrimination suffered by free blacks living in non-slave states. It had been a subject of great debate in the black community. Mary Ann believed in action, and looking to oneself to solve problems. Her letter didn't pull any punches. She criticized the community, and herself, for "whining over our difficulties and afflictions … We should do more, and talk less," she wrote.

To do more, Mary Ann took up her pen again that year, writing and publishing a pamphlet expressing her views on the oppression of African-Americans. "My destiny is that of my people," she wrote in *Hints to the Colored People of the North*. Because of this belief, she was willing to say anything – no matter whom it offended. She saw it as her duty to "expose every weakness" within the community, if she believed it held black people back. She denounced everything from the way some spent their money to the influence of church leaders. These were her first published writings; her critical style and strong opinions that she knew what was best would never change. One well-known black abolitionist said the pamphlet was "an excellent introduction to a great subject."

In 1850, the American government passed a law that put all black people in danger, in both slave and free states. The Fugitive Slave Act allowed slave owners to hunt down those who had escaped, anywhere in the country, and take them back into slavery. This put every black person at risk of being kidnapped and sold. Canada, where slavery had been abolished in 1833, began to look like the safest haven. Mary Ann also saw Canada as a place where her people could establish a whole new way of life. In 1851, she moved to the township of Windsor in Canada West, later called the province of Ontario.

The Term "Colored"

African-Americans' struggles for equality include changing the words used to describe them as a group. In the mid-1800s, the term "colored" was accepted by both black and white people, and was regarded as the most respectful. "Negro" became more common in the next century, and then was replaced by "black" and "African-American."

Mary Ann chose Windsor because she had met two black community leaders from that area. Henry Bibb and his wife, Mary, ran the first newspaper for black people in Canada, called *Voice of the Fugitive*. Mary Bibb was also a teacher, and she and Henry told Mary Ann that more teachers were needed. So Mary Ann started her own school. But her strong opinions soon brought her into conflict with the Bibbs. The Bibbs believed it was best for black children to have schools separate from whites. Mary Ann believed in teaching both races together; that's what she did in her school. The Bibbs thought living in Canada was a temporary solution for the black community. Mary Ann was convinced moving there permanently was their best chance for an equal society. Mary Ann and the Bibbs soon became fierce enemies. Many of their battles were fought in print.

Mary Ann wrote another pamphlet, this time to encourage African-Americans to move to Canada. But in it she also accused the Bibbs of discrimination against free black people. The Bibbs fought back. Their newspaper attacked and insulted Mary Ann, comparing her to the evil serpent that led to humankind's downfall in the Bible. Mary Ann kept up her own assault, writing a letter to *The Liberator* that said the Bibbs's newspaper "is not the voice of colored people in Canada," and that other voices needed to be heard. At this point, it's likely Mary Ann wanted her own newspaper – a much more powerful weapon than a pamphlet. In another letter, written privately, she complained, "I have not a paper of my own and must leave the result with God."

It wasn't like Mary Ann, however, to leave anything to anyone else, even God. In 1853, Mary Ann published the first edition of her own newspaper, called the *Provincial Freeman,* just one day after her school shut down for lack of funding. She created and published the paper, wrote for it, and edited it. But she didn't make her role public, because people in the

1800s would not have accepted a woman being in charge. Her name only appeared as the person to whom readers should write. A man named Samuel Ringgold Ward, an accomplished former slave, was named editor. Editors oversee all the material in a paper, and Ward had helped start other abolitionist publications, so his name gave the *Freeman* authority.

The newspaper's goals were clear in both its title and motto. The word "Freeman" created an image of someone strong and independent rather than someone running away, as suggested by the word "Fugitive" in the title of the Bibbs's paper. The word "Provincial" came from its location, outside the United States, where Mary Ann thought black people should be. The newspaper's motto was "Self-Reliance is the True Road to Independence." Mary Ann believed black people would get ahead if they did not rely on whites. The first edition also said the newspaper would not be influenced by any political party or religion.

A publisher's job includes looking after the business end of things, and after the first issue, Mary Ann spent a year raising money to keep the paper going. By 1854, she had what she needed and set up shop in Toronto, where she put out the *Freeman* on a weekly basis. The newspaper provided, in Mary Ann's words, "some cheap, reliable means of information furnished by persons on the spot" – one of the most basic roles of journalism. She and others reported on local events. But the paper had much more. It included investigative journalism, digging deep into the activities of organizations, such as a charity that was not doing what it promised for the community. There were articles about women's rights, which increasingly interested Mary Ann, and also debates about the best ways to fight slavery. Mary Ann wrote that if the *Provincial Freeman* survived, it would be an important means of "communication between the friends of the downtrodden." The *Freeman* was a way for people in a new country to talk to one another.

Especially important were letters from readers that sometimes took up a full page of the paper. It was a letter that finally made Mary Ann lose her temper about the lack of recognition for her work. Mary Ann was doing almost everything, but Ward was still listed as editor, even though he was mostly out of the country. When one letter written to "Mr." Shadd praised the "colored man" for putting the paper together, Mary Ann had had enough. She revealed she was a woman, and stopped pretending Ward was the editor; the work and the credit for it now fully belonged to her.

Sadly, this did not last long. The next year, Mary Ann announced she was stepping down from editing and named a new man to the post. It's not completely clear why she did this, but she believed "obnoxious persons" were against her because she was a woman, and the resulting criticism of the paper may have threatened its survival. There could have been other reasons the paper was criticized. Mary Ann had continued to anger people with her outspoken remarks. She blasted some letters to the paper as a "waste of time." She said she had "contempt" for black women who did not work hard enough for the anti-slavery cause. And she condemned some leaders of the abolitionist movement. Her belief that it was her duty to speak out must have cost her support.

Despite formally stepping

Following Mary Ann's Lead

Ida B. Wells-Barnett 1862 - 1931
The daughter of slaves. Best known for her crusade, through newspapers and pamphlets, against lynching. In a lynching, a mob of white people would capture a black man and hang him.

Ethel Payne 1911 - 1991
Reported on the civil rights movement in the U.S. in the 1950s and 1960s. Often referred to as the "first lady of the black press," she also covered Washington and international politics. The American government honored her with a postage stamp in 2002.

down, Mary Ann had taken an historic step by holding the editorial job; she had become the first black woman editor in North America. She wrote an inspiring message to black women, encouraging them to follow her lead. "To colored women ... we have 'broken the editorial ice' ... so go to Editing, as many of you are willing, and able."

After only about a year in Toronto, Mary Ann decided to move the *Freeman*. Her parents and other family were in Chatham, about 170 miles (300 km) away, and the area had a growing black population. "Go to Chatham," a black historian reported at the time, and "you'll see heaps of our people." There, Mary Ann's life changed dramatically. In 1856, at the age of thirty-two, she married. Her husband, Thomas Cary, was a financial supporter of Mary Ann's newspaper, a barbershop owner, and a widower with three children. Mary Ann became a stepmother and then a mother when her daughter, Sarah, was born the following year.

During the Chatham years, the *Provincial Freeman* was published only once in a while. There were money problems, and Mary Ann's time may have been more limited once she became a wife and mother. The exact date of when the *Freeman* ceased publication isn't known. The last surviving editorial written by Mary Ann is from June 1859, and the paper seems to have ended around 1860, seven years after Mary Ann started it.

That same year, personal and historical events changed Mary Ann's life yet again. In November 1860, her husband died. Thomas Cary was just thirty-five years old. Mary Ann was pregnant at the time with their second child, a son, Linton, who was born a few months later. In April 1861, the American Civil War began. In a civil war, people from the same country fight each other. In this case the fight was about slavery: the southern states believed in slavery and the northern states did not. In 1865, the North was victorious, and slavery ended.

About 20,000 slaves had escaped to Canada between the time of the Fugitive Slave Act and the beginning of the Civil War. After the war, many returned to the United States. By 1868, despite holding a Canadian passport and citizenship, Mary Ann decided to go back, too. She moved to Detroit and returned to teaching.

Mary Ann's accomplishments over the next twenty-five years were enough for another entire lifetime. She continued to write articles about racism and politics, and became more involved in women's rights. In 1880, she formed the Colored Women's Progressive Franchise Association to advance the cause of black women fighting for the right to vote. All men, white and black, were entitled to vote, after a change to the law following the Civil War. But voting was illegal for women of any race. Mary Ann also turned to law as a career and is reported

The Mary Ann Shadd Cary House in Washington, D.C.

Landmarks

The house where Mary Ann Shadd Cary lived in Washington, D.C. from 1881 to 1885 was declared a National Historic Landmark of the United States in 1976.

In Canada, Mary Ann was designated a Person of National Historic Significance. She has also been honored with several plaques in the Chatham area.

to have been the first African-American woman to enrol in an American law school. She was awarded her degree when she was sixty, and proudly advertised herself as M. A. Shadd Cary Esquire, "a colored lady lawyer."

Mary Ann Shadd Cary died in 1893, at the age of sixty-nine. During her lifetime, Frederick Douglass, an abolitionist and former slave, called her "a pioneer among colored women." Others spoke of her intelligence. She was also called eccentric. Mary Ann was indeed a very different kind of woman for her time. She believed that neither gender nor race should stop her from doing what she wanted – and usually they didn't. Her determination, her outrage at injustice, and the power of her written word blazed trails for others to follow. Today her contributions receive the credit they deserve, in books and monuments. But it took many decades before she began to receive widespread recognition. One can only imagine what Mary Ann would have said about that.

NELLIE BLY

"I'd rather go back to New York dead than not a winner."

1864 - 1922

Training elephants for the circus is not the usual kind of assignment for a newspaper reporter. For Nellie Bly, who had become famous for her worldwide adventures, it was just another experience to add to her long list of daring enterprises. But when she wrote about it later, Nellie revealed an aspect of her personality rarely seen. After the circus trainer told Nellie she had performed tricks with the elephants that even some professionals wouldn't try, Nellie wrote, "I did not tell him ... I merely did it because I hadn't courage to say I was afraid."

No one ever would have used the word "afraid" to describe Nellie Bly. She was known for her stunt journalism, reporting risky and exciting stories that held the public in awe –

particularly because she was a woman. It was always said she was courageous. But her bravery wasn't limited to wild exploits such as training elephants. She also stood up for people abused by society's injustice, expressed opinions far ahead of her time, and, along the way, fought for equality as a female journalist.

Nellie Bly was not her real name. She was born Elizabeth Jane Cochran on May 5, 1864, in Cochran's Mills, a small town in Pennsylvania that was named for her father. Michael Cochran was a judge and a successful businessman. Mary Jane, Elizabeth's mother, was Michael's second wife, and they had thirteen children between them. The Cochrans had a comfortable existence until Michael died suddenly, shortly after Elizabeth's sixth birthday, leaving the family with terrible money problems. That may have been the reason Mary Jane remarried just a few years later.

The new husband, John Ford, turned out to be an abusive, frightening man who would fly into rages and threaten to kill his wife. Once, he showed up drunk with a loaded pistol when Mary Jane was at a church event. Another time, Elizabeth and her brother jumped between their mother and Ford when he was attacking her. Despite the shame of divorce in those times, Mary Jane decided to end the marriage. Elizabeth was fourteen when she went to court to testify against her stepfather. Her testimony makes it clear how terrifying life was with him. "Ford has been generally drunk since they were married," she said. "Mother was afraid of him … The first time I seen [sic] Ford take hold of mother in an angry manner, he attempted to choke her."

The divorce was eventually granted, but the financial problems remained. Elizabeth went away to school to become a teacher, but had to leave because she could not afford the tuition. Two of her brothers had found work in Pittsburgh, so in 1880, when Elizabeth was sixteen, she, her mother, and two younger siblings moved to be with them. Pittsburgh was known as one of the dirtiest cities in the United States, and life there was hard. A writer of the time said it looked like "hell with the lid off."

For the next four years, not much is known about Elizabeth's life, although it's clear she couldn't find good, steady work. But at age twenty, with the writing of one angry letter, her fortunes changed.

In early 1885, Elizabeth read a series of columns about women's role in society, in *The Pittsburgh Dispatch* newspaper. The writer, Erasmus Wilson, called women who had jobs "a monstrosity" and "disgusting." He said women should get married and tend to household chores such as sewing, cooking, and raising children. Any woman who worked outside the home, he wrote, was taking away the rights given to men "by heaven" to have jobs.

Elizabeth and many other women were enraged. They knew women who desperately needed employment to help with family finances. Many worked at factory jobs that were poorly paid, dirty, and sometimes dangerous. Elizabeth wrote to the editor of the *Dispatch*, saying Wilson was wrong. She signed herself "Lonely Orphan Girl." Although she was not actually an orphan, it was a nice dramatic touch, and the letter caught the editor's attention. George Madden admired her spirit and the fact she gave her opinion "straight out." He asked Elizabeth to meet him, and when she did, decided to give her a try at the paper, even though her grammar was described as being a little "rocky."

Elizabeth's first story was about working women in Pittsburgh who didn't have enough money for food or heat. She attacked the rich for their lack of caring. She wrote next about divorce; she wanted the laws changed to make divorce easier to obtain. These were the kinds of stories Elizabeth would write throughout her career – about society's underdogs, and against popular opinion. After the second piece, Madden hired her full-time for a salary of $5 a week. This was an incredible accomplishment, given that women were rarely hired as reporters.

Now that she had a job, she needed a new name. It was the custom of the time that women writers would not use their own names. "Nelly Bly" was a popular American song in the 1800s, and someone in the newsroom thought it was a good name for Elizabeth. It was, and though the editor spelled it incorrectly, "Nellie Bly" was the name she used from this time on.

Madden soon assigned Nellie to the women's sections. She hated writing about things newspapers thought women cared about, such as gardening and hairstyles. After only nine

Nellie Bly's adventures would make her one of the famous women of her time.

months, she resigned her full-time job. "I was too impatient to work along at the usual duties assigned women on newspapers," she said. Nellie was determined to have more exciting work, and set off for Mexico to try her hand at foreign reporting.

She spent six months traveling in Mexico and wrote stories about all aspects of Mexican life. Her reports were published in the *Dispatch*, as well as in other American newspapers. Nellie then returned to Pittsburgh, and to a full-time job at her old newspaper. But she was assigned to cover theater and the arts. Although this was considered good work for a woman reporter, it was too tame for Nellie. In less than a year she was gone again, this time without saying good-bye. She only left a simple note: "I am off for New York. Look out for me. Bly."

New York was not an easy nut to crack, and Nellie spent months knocking on doors, trying to find reporting work. Eventually, she met an editor from the *New York World* newspaper, owned by Joseph Pulitzer. Today, Pulitzer is famous for the prize given as America's highest honor for journalism or literature. In the late 1800s, his newspaper and some others in New York were known for "yellow journalism" – a term used for sensational stories considered to have no real value. Except, of course, to sell papers.

New York World had an attention-grabbing idea for Nellie. The editor wanted her to pretend to be insane and get herself put away in the city's most notorious mental institution, the Women's Lunatic Asylum on Blackwell's Island. Then, after seeing it from the inside as a patient, she could write about it. Nellie agreed. She needed the money and felt the story would give her the chance to make a name for herself. Nellie also said she had a social purpose; she wanted to be sure that "the most helpless of God's creatures, the insane, were cared for kindly and properly."

She started the assignment by staying at a boarding house where she began to act as if she had lost her mind. The police were called, and she was soon locked away on Blackwell's Island. In total, she spent ten days there, experiencing terrible physical conditions and treatment. Then Pulitzer sent a lawyer to get her out.

Nellie's first report was headlined, "Behind Asylum Bars," and the second, "Inside the Madhouse." She wrote, "The insane asylum on Blackwell's Island is a human rat-trap. It is easy to get in, but once there it is impossible to get out ... I have watched patients stand and gaze longingly toward the city they in all likelihood will never enter again ... it seems so near, and yet heaven is not further from hell."

The stories were a huge success, and the sensation was as much about Nellie as it was about her reports. That a woman had willingly been imprisoned in a lunatic asylum astounded the public. The reports became one of the best-known examples of what was called "stunt" journalism – a craze in the late 1800s in the United States. Usually women did the stunts, as readers seemed to love reports of women doing things out of the ordinary. Again, that sold newspapers. Female stunt reporters put on disguises, or pretended to be something they weren't, to find things out. Sometimes, they took physical risks. Some people said the craze was vulgar, and thought women were demeaning

Stunt Journalists

Nellie Bly may have been the most famous, but she was not the only female stunt journalist. These stunts may seem tame today, but at the time they were very adventurous!

In 1894, Caroline Lockhart went to the bottom of Boston harbor in a diving suit. Another time, she wore bloomers – long pants worn under a dress, designed to give women more freedom – to see the public's reaction.

In 1896, Dorothy Dare was hailed as "the first woman to take a spin through the streets of New York in a horseless carriage." In other words, she rode in a car.

themselves. Others saw it as a way for women to enter the mostly male world of journalism, while at the same time doing society some good. As a result of Nellie's story on the asylum, for example, New York City agreed to substantially increase the money given to the institution so that the conditions she wrote about could be improved.

The stories made Nellie an instant star, something she didn't mind in the least. She loved being the center of attention and had a talent for this style of reporting. But Nellie also wanted to help people and expose society's wrongs. She posed as a maid and revealed that employment agencies cheated the servants working for them. Pretending she was an unmarried mother with an infant, she exposed the way newborn babies were being illegally sold for adoption. A colleague of Nellie's at *New York World* said her assets as a reporter were "courage, persistence and ... self-confidence."

A few years after Blackwell's Island, Nellie came up with an even bigger idea for getting attention. A French author named Jules Verne had written a popular book of fiction called *Around the World in 80 Days*. In an age when there were no airplanes, being able to travel around the globe this quickly seemed impossible. But Nellie said that she would do it – and in less than eighty days!

The newspaper's management liked the idea, but didn't want Nellie to do it. "It is impossible for you to do it," was the terrible verdict, Nellie wrote. "In the first place you are a woman and would need a protector, and even if it were possible for you to travel alone you would need to carry so much baggage that it would detain you in making rapid changes ... there is no use talking about it; no one but a man can do this." Nellie told them to go ahead and hire a man. She would go to another newspaper, do the stunt for them, and beat the man.

The newspaper's editors backed down. They wanted this story and knew that Nellie would likely do as she threatened.

On November 14, 1889, Nellie set sail from New Jersey, alone, and with just one piece of hand luggage to last her for three months. The American public followed her every move as she traveled as fast as was possible in those times. She journeyed by train, boat, and carriage, and cabled her stories back to the newspaper along the way. By Christmas, Nellie was in China. Then she set sail for Japan, but ran into horrendous storms that threatened to slow her down. Another woman was making the same trip, trying to beat Nellie at her own stunt. With her usual bravado, Nellie said, "I'd rather go back to New York dead than not a winner."

In January 1890, she landed in San Francisco and boarded a special train to take her across the country. At every stop, the crowds gathering to meet her grew larger and larger. Nellie arrived at the Jersey City train station on January 25: seventy-two days, six hours, and eleven minutes after she had left. Guns boomed their greetings, and people were said to have roared "with a thousand throats." Nellie Bly was only twenty-five at the time, but according to some, she was the most famous woman on Earth.

Around the World

Nellie wrote a book, *Around the World in 72 Days*, about her amazing trip. This excerpt leaves no doubt about her love of adventure: "The terrible swell of the sea during the monsoon was the most beautiful thing I ever saw. I would sit breathless on deck watching the bow of the ship standing upright on a wave then dash headlong down as if intending to carry us to the bottom."

Most people would have been scared stiff – or seasick. But not Nellie.

Over time, stunt journalism became less popular, and Nellie turned more often to other kinds of stories. She wrote about controversial issues, speaking out against capital punishment and reporting on the fight for women's right to vote. She interviewed activist Emma Goldman, who was in jail because of her radical political activities, about her goals to improve the lives of working people. She ended her report by praising Goldman as a "modern Joan of Arc."

Board game about journalist Nellie's trip around the world in 1889-1890 from *New York World.*

Some of Nellie's
Round-the-World
Stops
London, England
Amiens, France
Brindisi, Italy
Port Said, Egypt
Singapore
Hong Kong
Canton, China

In 1895, at age thirty, Nellie shocked everyone by marrying in typically dramatic fashion. Her husband was Robert Seaman, a sixty-nine-year-old millionaire businessman nearly forty years her senior. Nellie continued to do some work as a reporter, but also enjoyed a wealthy lifestyle and travel abroad. Less than ten years after the wedding, Seaman died, and Nellie ran his business for a while. But it eventually failed, partly because some employees, including a good friend, stole hundreds of thousands of dollars.

Nellie went back to reporting, going overseas to cover the conflicts of World War I and then later, at home, leading public crusades to improve the welfare of orphans. Over a journalistic career spanning thirty-seven years, she never lost what one colleague called her "kindness of heart."

Nellie Bly died in 1922, of bronchopneumonia and heart disease. She was fifty-seven years old. Her obituary in *The New York Times* spoke of her "courage and liveliness." Arthur Brisbane, a friend and columnist, wrote, "reporting requires intelligence, precision, honesty of purpose, courage and accuracy ... Nellie Bly was the best reporter in America." There were many glowing tributes, but Nellie died with little money and was buried in an unmarked grave at Woodlawn Cemetery in the Bronx. Nearly sixty years later, in 1978, the New York Press Club erected a memorial there for her. Under her name, it says simply, "In honor of a famous news reporter."

MARGARET BOURKE-WHITE

"I simply cannot bear being away from things that happen."

1904 - 1971

When Margaret Bourke-White was a girl, she kept snakes as pets. The creatures that other children usually find creepy, she thought were wonderful. She had a whole collection: garter snakes she found in her yard; a baby boa constrictor her father bought her; and one called a puff adder. It wasn't poisonous, but would puff itself up and scare everyone. Margaret was proud of her snakes and took them to school to show them off. Not surprisingly, the principal demanded she take them home.

Many years later, Margaret said that as a child she had decided she would do "all the things women never do." Certainly, collecting snakes gave her an early start toward achieving this goal. As an adult, she became a photojournalist – someone who reports news events by using photographs rather than words. It was an entirely new profession in the twentieth century, and Margaret was not only one of the first, but she also continues to be one of the most famous photojournalists of all time. She photographed wars and disasters, was nearly killed in an enemy attack that sank her ship, witnessed some of the world's worst horrors, and met some of its greatest and poorest people. Margaret Bourke-White seems to have gone almost everywhere and photographed almost every major historic event of her time.

It is perhaps not surprising that Margaret's parents should have had such a unique daughter. Her mother, Minnie Bourke, was from an Irish-Catholic family. Her father, Joseph White, had been raised in an Orthodox Jewish family, although he eventually rejected all religion. Their marriage in 1898 was unusual; society did not approve of Christians and Jews marrying. But Joseph and Minnie were well suited. They didn't care what others thought, and they passed this mindset and many other progressive views – including a belief in the equal value of women's work – on to their children.

Margaret was born June 14, 1904, in the Bronx in New York, the second child of three. Minnie is said to have been creative in the ways she taught her children. When Margaret was young, for example, she was terrified of being alone in the dark. Her mother helped her by playing a running game outside. Each night, when darkness fell, Minnie encouraged her daughter to run farther and farther, circling around the house by herself. Eventually, Margaret overcame her fears – a lesson she would call on time and again during the many dangerous situations she faced while on assignments. Her mother also encouraged curiosity. "Mother would say, 'Open all the doors,'" Margaret wrote.

Margaret's father was an engineer and inventor who

worked at a factory. He had a great love of machines and taught his daughter that they were just as beautiful as any work of nature. Joseph's hobby was photography, and his photographs of the family, birds, and flowers hung in their home. When Margaret became a photographer years later, she would first achieve fame with her wonderfully creative shots of machinery. But it was the high standards he set – to do a job "better than anyone else requires you to do it" – that Margaret would later credit for her success.

Margaret went to Columbia University in New York when she was seventeen. She still loved snakes and planned to become a herpetologist – a scientist who studies reptiles and amphibians. Just a few months after she started school, her father died of a stroke. It was a devastating blow. When she returned to university classes, she also signed up for a course in her father's hobby, photography, for two hours a week at the Clarence H. White School. Clarence White (he was not related to Margaret) was said to be a brilliant teacher of both technique and design. Margaret used her new skills to get a job as a photography counselor at a summer camp. When she

The Image of Beauty

When Margaret Bourke-White was a child, her father took her to visit steel foundries – places where metal is melted. She never forgot the wonder of it. "To me at that age, a foundry represented the beginning and end of all beauty," she later wrote. It "was so vivid and alive that it shaped the whole course of my career."

wasn't teaching the children, she was demonstrating her dedication to getting the right shot, staying up all night to catch the sunrise on film, or climbing to the edge of a cliff to capture a view of the steep drop.

About a year after her father's death, Margaret began dating a man named Everett Chapman, and they married on June 13, 1924, one day before Margaret's twentieth birthday. Things went wrong from the beginning, when Everett's mother joined them on their honeymoon. Mrs. Chapman's interference, along with other problems, brought the marriage to an end after two years. Margaret would later say she felt an odd debt of gratitude to her former mother-in-law for making her life so miserable. She said it taught her strength and the breakup put her on the path to a new life.

Margaret didn't finish her biology degree until 1927, because she had had to move many times for her husband's work. But by this time photography had become more important to her than science; after graduation, she moved to Cleveland to open a photography studio. When she started her career, she also changed her last name to Bourke-White, using both her parents' surnames. She had never liked being called by her husband's last name when she was married, and her new name gave her a fresh start.

Cleveland was one of America's largest cities, and its manufacturing businesses were booming. Inspired by her father's vision of machines as beautiful objects, she took striking photographs of industry – the blades of a plow, chimney stacks, and steel factories became works of art through Margaret's camera lens. Her reputation grew quickly, and two years later one of the world's most powerful media men, Henry Luce, came calling. He hired Margaret as the first photographer for a new magazine called *Fortune*, about the world of business and the economy. Margaret told many dramatic stories through her pictures for the magazine. In Germany, she shot images of the country rebuilding after the devastation of World War I. She became the first foreigner to photograph the results of the Soviet Union's rapid industrialization plans. The Soviet Union was known for being a closed country, but Margaret was incredibly persistent and was finally let in to do her work. "Nothing," she said, "attracts me like a closed door." Her photographs from the Soviet Union resulted in *Eyes on Russia*, the first of Margaret's nine books.

In 1934, Margaret was sent on an assignment that profoundly changed her approach to life and work. There had been a devastating lack of rain in a huge area of the United States, which became known as the "Dust Bowl" because farmland had literally become dust. Crops couldn't grow and cattle had no food. It was also the era of the Great Depression; people had no work and no money. Confronting human tragedy for the first time, Margaret wrote that she had "never seen people caught helpless like this." She was no longer a photographer trying to get the best picture of a thing, an object. She focused instead on the farmers and their families. "Suddenly, it was the people who counted ... I saw everything in a new light." After this, her photographs of people's faces would bring Margaret the most fame. But in 1934, these faces also brought her a new awareness of suffering and injustice. She began supporting causes that improved people's lives and, from this point on, spoke out on behalf of people she saw who were oppressed.

At about the same time, Henry Luce was developing a new magazine in which photographs – not words – would be the main source of information. It was a revolutionary idea, and Luce hired Margaret to help make it happen. The first issue of *Life* came out in 1936. A photograph by Margaret was on the cover, and she was the only woman photographer featured in that issue. Most important, though, were Margaret's images of a boomtown that had sprung up near the construction site of a giant dam. She put the photographs together as

Self-portrait, 1943. Margaret's many accomplishments included being the first woman authorized to fly a combat mission with the U.S. Forces in World War II.

a series, in a way that told a story without needing words. This series of pictures was an entirely new form of journalism that became known as a photo essay, and Margaret's was the first in America. *Life* was an immediate success. Together, Margaret and the magazine would become known around the world for photographs of some of the greatest figures and historic events of the 1900s.

In 1941, the United States joined World War II and the battle against Germany and Japan. Margaret was the first woman given permission to photograph the war. She was thrilled. Her husband was not. Two years earlier, despite misgivings that marriage took away a woman's independence, she had remarried. Erskine Caldwell was a famous author she met when they worked together on a book. While Margaret was urging women to get involved with the war effort, saying she doubted "there had ever been a war in history where women could play such a vital part," Caldwell was saying he wanted her home. She was on assignment in England in 1942 when Caldwell wrote from America to say their marriage was over. She later told a friend there had already been many problems in the marriage, but also said she was not willing to leave her war assignments as he had asked. "In a world like this I simply cannot bear being away from things that happen" – an apt definition of a journalist if ever there was one. "It would be a mistake for me not to be recording the march of events with my camera."

During the war, Margaret also became the first woman authorized to fly on a combat bombing mission. But the risks of war became most real in December 1942 when Margaret was traveling to Africa to cover battles with Germany on that continent. Her ship was carrying more than six thousand troops and hundreds of nurses when it was hit by a torpedo and began to sink. She wrote afterwards that she had never been in such danger, or so afraid. But she was also inspired by the courage of ordinary people who helped others and worked together to get as many people as possible to safety. It had "a profound effect on my understanding and feeling toward other human beings," she wrote. Sometimes, when she wrote like this, Margaret still sounded like a scientist, except now her discoveries were about the qualities of being human.

As the war was ending in Europe in 1945, Margaret photographed the worst scenes of horror she would experience, ones she said were "more than the mind could grasp." The Nazis had built concentration camps throughout the war. These camps had two purposes: to kill large numbers of people, and to imprison others and make them work as slaves. The camps were for people the Nazis hated: mostly Jews, but also other groups that the Nazis considered their enemies, or inferior. Millions of people were killed. Those who weren't murdered were starved and tortured. Margaret was traveling with American troops when they arrived at Buchenwald concentration camp. There, she took photographs of the piles of dead bodies, and haunting pictures of the survivors. These photographs were used as evidence in trials of captured Nazi leaders after the war. Margaret wanted to remind the world – through

Photographing the War

In 1941, Margaret Bourke-White was the only foreign photographer in Russia's capital, Moscow, when Germany began to bomb the city. She went to the roof of the American embassy to photograph the attack. Margaret was so caught up in capturing the flashing lights, planes, and falling bombs on film, she had no sense of danger. Later, she called it "one of the outstanding nights of my life."

her images – that people "had performed these horrors because of race prejudice and hatred."

After the war, Margaret continued to work for *Life* anywhere in the world where history was being made. One of her most famous photographs was of the great Indian leader Mahatma Gandhi, who was fighting for his country's independence by using non-violent protest. She traveled to South Africa where a system called apartheid gave white people all the power, while black Africans and other non-whites were treated cruelly. Some of them worked in inhumane conditions in gold mines, and one of Margaret's photographs, of two black miners sweating in the horrible heat underground, became a symbol of injustice. Margaret said it was one of her favorite photographs.

> "My life and my career was not an accident. It was thoroughly thought out."
> —Margaret Bourke-White in an interview, 1960

In 1952, at the age of forty-eight, Margaret was photographing the Korean War when she began to have problems with her hands and arms. She was eventually diagnosed with Parkinson's disease, a disorder that affects the brain and causes loss of control of movement. It gets progressively worse over time. She didn't tell anyone she was ill, but it became hard to hide, and after 1957 she could no longer carry out assignments for *Life*. She did continue to take photographs, though, and also wrote her autobiography, *Portrait of Myself*, which became a bestseller in 1963. The illness affected her speech and balance, but Margaret always had a knack for looking at life's difficulties in a positive way. In a letter to a friend, she said that having the condition was "one of the great experiences" of her life. "It brought me closer to other human beings in a way I cannot put into words." Margaret fought her disease past the point at which many would have given up.

But on August 27, 1971, after a fall at her home, she died. She was sixty-seven.

Over her lifetime and beyond, Margaret Bourke-White had a huge impact on the way people learn about and understand world events, and she advanced the art of photography with great creativity. Photographers, she said in her autobiography, "see a great deal of the world. Our obligation is to pass it on to others." Margaret was a pioneer who set many milestones in a completely new area of journalism, and in a media world dominated by men. Today, her photographs hang in some of America's best museums, and her work is the subject of many books. "She was always reaching beyond, trying to better what she had done," one colleague said after her death. "Margaret was one of the great achievers of our time."

Seeing Margaret's Work Online

Margaret Bourke-White's photographs can be seen in many museums. Here are a few you can visit online.

The Art Institute of Chicago
http://www.artic.edu/aic/

The Cleveland Museum of Art
http://www.clemusart.com/

Harvard Art Museum
http://www.artmuseums.harvard.edu/

Los Angeles County Museum of Art
http://www.lacma.org/

The Metropolitan Museum of Art, New York
http://www.metmuseum.org/

The Phillips Collection
http://www.phillipscollection.org/

San Francisco Museum of Modern Art
http://www.sfmoma.org/

DORIS ANDERSON

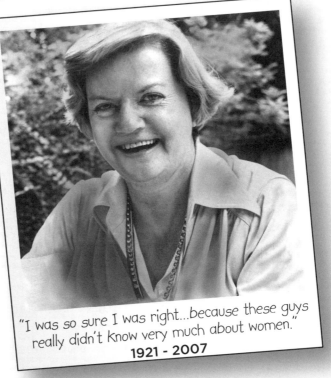

"I was so sure I was right...because these guys really didn't know very much about women."

1921 - 2007

Doris Anderson grew up in a world where girls and women were supposed to keep quiet. Doris didn't want to be quiet. In her house when she was growing up, and in most homes of that time, men were in charge and made all the decisions. Doris thought that was stupid. Girls and women weren't supposed to want careers; they were expected to get married. Doris rebelled against that. She believed that these and many of the other so-called rules about how women should live their lives were wrong. She was determined to help change them. And she did – through her journalism and her rebellious spirit, Doris Anderson was one of those people who actually changed the world.

She was born Hilda Doris Buck in the province of Alberta, in Canada, on November 10, 1921. Her mother was not married, which, according to society at the time, meant that Doris was an "illegitimate" child. This was considered shameful, so Doris's mother, Rebecca Buck, put her in a home for unwanted babies. But Doris became weak and sickly, and after a few months Rebecca changed her mind and took her child home to the city of Calgary. There, the baby became well, and grew up happily enough until she was nearly eight years old.

That's when Rebecca married the man who was Doris's father. His name was Thomas McCubbin, and he had been living for many years in the boarding house run by Doris's mother and grandmother. Doris did not like her father. He was a quarrelsome man with a drinking problem and no job. Yet just because he was a man, he was in charge. Doris hated it. She said that her mother had been running their lives very well on her own. Then, suddenly, her father was making all the rules, and "they were stupid rules." Her parents had two more children, both boys. But it was a very difficult marriage; in later years, one of Doris's brothers said their home "wasn't for the faint of heart." It was made worse by the father's drunkenness, which Doris despised. "I fervently wanted my father to be hit by a streetcar, particularly when … he reeled in late, three sheets to the wind." Doris had to learn to stand up for herself early, a good friend said later, or she would have been crushed by the misery at home.

As well as hating her father, Doris was angry with her mother. Rebecca was trying to raise her daughter to do what she had done: obey men, get married, and settle down. This was not the life Doris wanted. She loved school and did well at her studies. When she was eighteen, she began work as a teacher to earn money to go to university. One of her aunts congratulated her for this – not because she was going to get a better education, but because Doris would then meet a better man to marry. Many people thought that was the only reason for women to go to university.

Doris had seen from her parents' marriage what could happen to a woman's life, and she was not the least bit interested in having that happen to her. She put herself through school at the University of Alberta, graduating with her Bachelor of Arts degree in 1945. After that she left her home province, first going to the city of Toronto in central Canada, and then traveling to England, where she tried to develop a career writing fiction. She did sell some work, but realized she could not make enough money and returned to Toronto. When she had lived there before, she had tried to follow her dream of becoming a journalist, but couldn't get a job. Now, she was hired by *Chatelaine* magazine to do some low-level advertising work. It wasn't journalism, but once she had her foot in the door, there was no holding Doris back. She was about to fight her way right to the top.

In 1951, at the time Doris started working at *Chatelaine*, she was almost thirty years old. *Chatelaine* had been publishing for more than twenty years. It was a women's magazine, and its articles were mostly about cooking, fashion, and families. Doris thought it could and should include so much more than that, because women's interests were changing.

Once she worked her way up to being a writer, she fought with the editor, John Clare, about these issues. He thought the magazine was fine the way it was. Doris was absolutely convinced that he and the other male managers had no idea what women really wanted to read about. "I was so sure I was right ... because these guys really didn't know very much about women."

Despite the disputes, Doris was promoted and by 1956 was managing editor. As editor, Clare was the boss; he was responsible for the magazine over all and had final say in all decisions. As managing editor, Doris was second-in-command, having a hand in most things, including the content of articles. In 1957, Clare left his job because of health problems, and the position of editor became available – just two weeks before Doris was to be married.

Her fiancé was a lawyer named David Anderson. While she still had doubts about marriage, Doris wanted children, and she was almost thirty-six years old. Because she was getting married, however, the men running the company that owned *Chatelaine* did not consider Doris for the editor's job. The company president, Floyd Chalmers, told Doris another man would be hired. He was astonished when Doris told him she would quit if that was the case. "But," Chalmers said, "you are going to be married and you will become a hostess and a mother." He could not believe a married woman would still want to work! Doris didn't back down. She insisted she was the best person to be editor. She got the job – although not everyone, including her future husband, was happy about it.

Doris then began the work she'd been dying to do ever since she started at *Chatelaine* – change it. Women's roles were becoming dramatically different. In the 1940s, men had gone away to fight in World War II. That meant women took jobs outside the home, earning their own money and becoming more independent. After the war, much of society thought women should go back to staying at home and being dependent on men. But many women wanted more than that, and Doris wanted those women as readers. She began to aim the content of *Chatelaine* at them. She kept the articles about food, family, and fashion, but also addressed many other issues.

In this respect, Doris and *Chatelaine* were far, far ahead of anyone else in the women's magazine business in North America. No subject was off-limits or too controversial. *Chatelaine* looked at laws that were unfair to women, such as those on divorce, or women's salaries. It was difficult to obtain a divorce in Canada at this time, and women often received poor financial settlements. In the workplace, women frequently earned half the amount or less than men would earn for the same work. As editor, Doris would also write about the lack of women in some professions, such as politics, or science, and about the extremely controversial issue of abortion laws.

Some readers were offended by the changes in the magazine, but many loved them. And they weren't just working women. For women isolated in their work as housewives, *Chatelaine* was creating a community of ideas. It was a place where they could read and talk about the world at large. This is what one subscriber wrote after controversial articles had some readers cancelling their subscriptions:

"Please! Please! Do not pay too much attention ... Please go on printing articles that keep us thinking ...

"What if I am mad with the author – I have a good argument with him while I wash dishes and make beds ... I hope you are making money and can stand the cancelled subscriptions. I'll never cancel mine until you start filling your good magazine with nothing but taffy recipes and a bunch of sweet stuff!"

Pregnant Women and Work

In 1958, Doris was pregnant with her first child. The company that owned *Chatelaine* had a policy that expectant mothers had to quit by the fifth month of their pregnancy. The managers did not make Doris leave, but they did make her work at home rather than the office. Doris thought this was ridiculous and refused to do it during her second pregnancy. By 1963, when she had her third child, the company policy was gone.

By 1959, one in every three English-speaking women in Canada was reading *Chatelaine*. With Doris Anderson at its head, the magazine had become a champion for women's rights. Some historians say it helped bring about the revolution called "second-wave feminism." The first wave of feminists, in the late 1800s and early 1900s, fought for women's right to vote. Second-wave feminists like Doris, in the latter 1950s and into the 1960s, were trying to change laws, as well as society's attitudes.

Doris and *Chatelaine* were also developing and changing the world of journalism. Doris discovered and hired some of the best female journalists in the country. Barbara Frum, who became one of Canada's best-known radio and television journalists, wrote for *Chatelaine* earlier in her career. Adrienne Clarkson, who also became a famous TV journalist, and later Canada's Governor General, wrote the magazine's book column. Doris also hired feminist Michele Landsberg, who continued to do groundbreaking work as a writer for national newspapers after her time at *Chatelaine*. June Callwood,

Working Mothers

For women who had children, the right to work was a huge and controversial debate in the 1950s and 1960s. Doris wrote in her autobiography that sometimes the worst attacks came from women. "At a party ..." she wrote, "I would occasionally be backed into a corner by a complete stranger. 'Why aren't you home looking after your children?' she would snarl."

known and loved for her work as a social activist, was another *Chatelaine* writer. And there were many more. Doris helped create a whole new generation of women journalists.

By 1969, Doris had been in charge of *Chatelaine* for twelve years. Her bosses said her magazine was by far the best run in the company. In her time as editor, she had increased the number of readers from less than 500,000 to 1.8 million. *Chatelaine* was making

> **A Reader's Letter from the 1960s**
>
> "I came to Canada from Germany eight years ago where my sister and her friends are just as engaged as we are here in questions such as, 'Should married women work outside their homes? in politics, etc?' ... a magazine like yours is so important in giving moral support ..."

money. Meanwhile, the weekly newsmagazine *Maclean's*, owned by the same company, Maclean Hunter, was losing money, though it was highly regarded for the quality of its journalism. When the job as *Maclean's* editor became available, Doris wanted a new challenge and thought she deserved it. Instead, a man was hired. Doris was sure she didn't get the job because of prejudice against her as a woman, and because she ran a women's magazine that didn't fit the male management's image of journalism. She said not getting the job was a "real kick in the face." By 2009, forty years after Doris was rejected, *Maclean's* had still never had a woman as its top editor.

> **Salary Discrimination**
>
> In 1969, running a successful magazine, Doris Anderson was making $23,000 a year. The man running *Maclean's*, which was not successful financially, made more than twice her salary: $53,000 a year.

Despite her anger at Maclean Hunter's management, Doris decided to stay at *Chatelaine*. As she wrote

One of Doris Anderson's later books
was about women's rights in other countries.

later, "a crisis far more serious … was taking place in my life." Her marriage was in trouble. Doris and her husband finally divorced in 1972, after three sons and fifteen years of marriage.

Five years later, in 1977, Doris hit her twenty-year mark as editor of *Chatelaine*. It was time for a move, especially as she had become deeply unhappy at Maclean Hunter. She resigned and took some time to travel and think about her future. In two decades as editor, she had helped change the way women were treated both at work and at home, and had been years ahead of anyone else in writing about women's issues. The famous American feminist magazine called *Ms.* did not appear in the United States until 1971. *Chatelaine* had been covering important women's issues for nearly fifteen years by then.

Leaving *Chatelaine* was certainly not the end of Doris Anderson's fight for women's rights. In 1978, she took her own advice – that women should be more involved in politics – and ran for office as a federal member of Parliament. She lost, but a year later the Canadian government appointed her as chair of the Canadian Advisory Council on the Status of Women, which informed the public and government about women's concerns. In the early 1980s, she took on a fight that may have been the most significant of her life. The government was creating a new legal document called the Charter of Rights and Freedoms. Anderson and many others believed this document did not do enough to protect women. Following Doris's lead, women across the country organized a protest and went to Canada's capital city of Ottawa. Eventually, the law's wording was changed, and now the rights of every Canadian woman are protected by it.

Doris continued working as a journalist for many years and wrote three novels, her autobiography, and columns for the *Toronto Star* newspaper. She received many honors, including one of the country's highest, as Companion of the Order of Canada.

Doris Anderson died at age eighty-five in Toronto on March 2, 2007. In her autobiography, *Rebel Daughter,* she wrote, "what I wanted more than anything was to be able to look after myself and make sure that every other woman in the world could do the same." She went a long way toward achieving that goal. Her work changed attitudes, laws, and bettered the lives of women in both the workplace and the home.

In her later years, Doris was concerned that a lot of women took their rights for granted and had "forgotten what it was like" for the generations of women who had struggled before them. Shortly after her death, a student at one of Canada's top journalism schools wrote a tribute to her in the *Ryerson Review of Journalism.* "I'm struck," she said, "by how journalists my age are oblivious to Doris Anderson's accomplishments. It is only because of such early feminists that my generation can do whatever we want ... we owe her a lot."

To this woman who refused to stay quiet, every woman in Canada could say the same.

BARBARA FRUM

"I get like a ferocious tiger."

1937 - 1992

When Barbara Frum was six years old, she asked for a pony. Her mother said no, but she knew her daughter always wanted to be given a reason. Florence said later that she shouldn't have done it, but she made one up. She told Barbara the neighbors wouldn't like it. Barbara went away, but returned later with a paper signed by all the neighbors saying they didn't mind if she had a pony. Determined to find out for herself if people thought a pony was a problem, Barbara had gone up and down the street and asked them.

Although Barbara didn't get her pony, she did get a bicycle. Her family loves to tell this story because it says a lot about the kind of person she was. Even from a young age, she was extraordinarily curious and dedicated to finding things out. As a journalist, she became famous for asking all kinds of questions of all kinds of people. And because she never backed down or gave up trying to find out the truth in the thousands and thousands of interviews she did over two decades, Barbara Frum was both loved and respected by her audience.

Barbara had to learn determination and discipline almost from the day she was born. During her birth on September 8, 1937, the doctor used an instrument that badly damaged her shoulder muscle. Until she was three years old, she had to wear an uncomfortable brace that held her arm in the air. It was supposed to heal the muscle, but it didn't work, and Barbara was never able to use her right arm properly, even to write or shake hands. Still, her mother never let her think there was anything wrong with her, or that there was anything she couldn't do. Barbara was sent to piano and dance lessons, the same as other children.

Both Barbara's parents were children of Jews who had immigrated to North America. Her father, Harold Rosberg, ran a family-owned department store in the small town of Niagara Falls, Canada. After Barbara, Harold and Florence had two more children. Barbara did well in school, although later she said she was the kind of student who "got E for effort" rather than one who had a natural talent for academics. She went on to study history at the University of Toronto. There, she met Murray Frum, a dentist. After eight months, and just a few days before her twentieth birthday, Barbara and Murray married. Their daughter later said that her mother's marriage was Barbara's "greatest accomplishment, the source of her largest joy."

Barbara finished her degree after she married, and she and Murray had two children: David and Linda. Barbara didn't consider having a career. "Nobody can believe it," she later told a writer. "I was blissfully happy ... I had never thought about a job." This was not unusual for women of that time. As Barbara explained to a high school audience after she had become a famous journalist, "It was able, ambitious young men the world was waiting for ... to be the future leaders of Canada ... We were to be their wives ... it occurred to almost none of us that we could make a name for ourselves."

It was her husband and her mother who encouraged Barbara to find work outside the home. She began volunteering for charities, and that led to writing for magazines and newspapers. Murray said Barbara did not have a goal in mind. "She never got up one morning and said, I'm going to be a journalist ... Each project led to the next." Another journalist said when she first met Barbara in these early years, her impression was of someone who was extremely smart, and who had an enthusiasm "that was very contagious." These qualities helped launch Barbara into the broadcast world.

In the 1960s, the women on TV information programs were often pretty blondes who were expected to have a soft approach and leave the hard material to the men. But when a producer from the Canadian Broadcasting Corporation met Barbara, he wanted to hire her. Besides being intelligent, Barbara could be direct and tough, and the producer thought she would attract viewers' attention. He hired her as one of seven hosts for his new program, *The Way It Is*. The six other hosts were men. One TV critic named her the best new interviewer of 1968. But when she moved to co-host another news program, management at CBC was uncomfortable with some of the questions Barbara asked; they wanted her to be friendlier. The interviews were about serious and controversial issues, and Barbara knew what a journalist's job was. It wasn't to be friendly. She always said she hoped she treated people politely, but her job was to find out the truth. The bosses eventually reduced her role on the program, and Barbara quit.

As it turned out, quitting was the best thing she could

have done. A few years earlier, CBC Radio had created a new program called *As It Happens*. Every night, Monday to Friday, it brought the world to Canadians through a simple technique: interviewing people on the telephone. It is commonplace now, but it was revolutionary at the time. Using the telephone meant radio could bring people up-to-the-minute information about news events "as they happened." In 1971, CBC hired Barbara as one of two *As It Happens* hosts. Later, she became the program's sole interviewer.

Barbara's personality and style broke the mold for what people thought women could do on air. Women did not read news or host programs on CBC radio then, so it was a big change for the audience, and sometimes for the people being interviewed. A hockey team owner she questioned about the poor performance of his players said, "females on the radio are a joke." He would only talk to the male sports reporter on the program. When Barbara kept asking questions, he told her to "keep quiet," and then hung up on her. Barbara won a national award that year as best radio interviewer, and humorously thanked the man who had insulted her.

Barbara's humor was part of what won her an audience. The majority of her interviews were about serious subjects: people in war zones, victims of tragedy, or those who had

Hear and See Barbara

CBC's website has radio and television clips of Barbara's best-known work in a section titled, Barbara Frum: Pioneering Broadcaster. You can hear and see her interviews, including the ones with the hockey team owner, and the cabbage farmer, at http://archives.cbc.ca/lifestyle/pastimes/topics/368-2087/

cheated the public or committed a crime. But *As It Happens* also did a lot of fun and even silly stories, and Barbara had a great knack for them. She interviewed an assortment of quirky people, such as the man who grew the world's biggest cabbage, and the man looking for people to help launch him across a river using a giant rubber slingshot. The audience loved these items, and so did Barbara, who would let loose with a rich, delighted laugh.

But it was Barbara's absolute determination to get answers in the serious interviews that the audience depended on and respected. Some guests tried to avoid her questions, or even lied. "I get like a ferocious tiger when that happens," Barbara said, "and I think that drives me." Her interviews were so important to Canadians who wanted to be well informed,

> "I cannot stand being bluffed or maneuvered or fooled or played with ... I hate falseness and I hate a lie."
> -Barbara Frum

and her name was so well known, that listeners would say, "I heard it on Barbara Frum last night."

By the fall of 1974, Barbara was thirty-six years old and had a wonderful marriage and a fulfilling family life. She and Murray now had three children, after adopting a baby boy, Matthew. Then Barbara went for a routine medical checkup, and the doctor discovered a lump under her arm. She had leukemia: a cancer of cells in the blood. One doctor said she had less than a year to live. Another said she might live for five more years. Barbara's father had died from the same disease just a few years before this, and only a few months after he was diagnosed. But Barbara and Murray made a decision; they would not stop their lives for this illness. "None of us knows how long we have on this earth," Murray told her. "Life's for living, and that's what we're going to do."

Barbara believed that if the public knew she had a life-threatening illness, it would destroy her ability to do her job properly. People would only think of her as a sick person, not as a journalist. She was also afraid that if her interview guests knew, they would feel sorry for her, and wouldn't answer her questions in a normal way. Her son David said she didn't want to be known as "Barbara Frum, dying person." Some journalists did find out about her illness but, understanding how it would affect Barbara's work, they didn't report it.

Despite her leukemia, Barbara continued life at a fierce pace. She loved her job and believed it helped keep her alive. A writer once asked her what she liked to do to relax. "I don't do anything to relax," she said. "I don't want to relax." On vacations, the Frums would travel to places Barbara wanted to know more about, because of her work. Barbara and Murray were passionate about collecting art, and Barbara became an enthusiastic gardener. She said it was "the perfect hobby for a compulsive personality." She read extensively, especially history. Her friends say she was extraordinarily devoted to them.

Barbara had been host of *As It Happens* for ten years when the man who had been her executive producer asked her to host a new program called *The Journal*. It would be like *As It Happens,* with Barbara interviewing people from around the world five nights a week, but it would be on television. Mark Starowicz showed her the huge TV studio they would work in. To his dismay, she said no. The woman who was fearless in interviews thought the technology was too overwhelming. Starowicz told her she would miss out on a huge and historic opportunity if she didn't take the job, and that eventually convinced her.

The Journal went to air for the first time on January 11, 1982, with Barbara and Mary Lou Finlay as hosts. Some say it was the first program in the world to have two women as anchors, rather than a man and a woman. Barbara's schedule became even more grueling. She often worked thirteen hours a day in order to be on top of all the research for interviews. They covered subjects as wide-ranging and complicated as crises in the Middle East, the assassination of India's prime minister, and the famous case of a Canadian Olympic athlete who won a gold medal, but was later discovered to have taken illegal drugs.

Working a daily program was chaotic and stressful, but Barbara was brilliant at it. If there were Canadians who didn't know Barbara Frum before, it is hard to believe there was anyone in the country who didn't know her now. *The Journal* also included award-winning documentaries, but for many it was the Barbara Frum show – that's who they were there to watch. More than one million viewers tuned in each night. Even the children's program *Sesame Street* had a character called "Barbara Plum" who was a TV reporter.

Barbara interviewed Canadian prime ministers, former American presidents, and high-ranking politicians and news-makers from around the world. Occasionally, there were

Barbara's Interview Secrets

One day Barbara Frum asked her daughter if she would like to know her secrets for doing good interviews. Linda was very excited, because her mother had never shared her techniques with anyone. She was prepared to spend a full day taking notes at this special meeting. Then Barbara said, "Use as few words as possible to ask your questions and then get out of the way." "That's it?" Linda asked. "That's it," her mother replied. "... Do this and you'll do a good job."

The Barbara Frum Atrium in Toronto's CBC building.

famous entertainers, such as former Beatle Paul McCartney. But in 2,600 editions of *The Journal*, the interviews she most appreciated were with people who had survived some kind of ordeal with grace and nobility. These included plane crash survivors, and a woman falsely accused of murder. Of all the people she interviewed, Nelson Mandela was one of the most memorable to her. Mandela fought for human rights and freedoms in his country of South Africa, where a system called apartheid gave a minority of white people the power, and the majority of black people almost none. Mandela was jailed for twenty-seven years. In 1990, he was released, and Barbara went to South Africa to meet him. She was tremendously moved and inspired by his dignity and lack of ill will toward the people who had treated him so badly.

By the spring of 1992, Barbara had been host of *The Journal* for ten years. She was still being treated for leukemia, but it had been nearly eighteen years since her diagnosis. That March, Barbara interviewed one of Canada's best-known authors, Mordecai Richler, and he and the audience could see something was wrong. Barbara was very sick, and went right to hospital after work. A few weeks later, just past midnight on March 26th, she died. Barbara was fifty-four years old.

The country was in shock. Barbara had been part of so many Canadians' daily lives for so long – nearly twenty-one years. And since most people hadn't known about her illness, her death seemed sudden. One article called it "a death in the family." The Canadian prime minister said it was "an enormous loss." Barbara was lauded as the "leading broadcaster of her generation," and her contribution as a role model for women

> "Barbara was not the model of a television host. Barbara was the model of a person."
> -Max Allen, former *As It Happens* producer

journalists was praised. Barbara's family was overwhelmed by the letters they received from the public; her daughter said it demonstrated how deeply meaningful her mother's life was to the country and its people.

Barbara Frum did not set out to be a journalist, and she had no intention of becoming famous. Instead, she wanted to fulfill the values she had been taught as a child – what she called an "extreme requirement to achieve." To her, that meant making a contribution. During her career, she won many awards, including the National Press Club of Canada Award for Outstanding Contribution to Canadian Journalism, and the Order of Canada, the country's highest civilian honor. As a measure of her historic contribution, Canada's national archives selected her *As It Happens* interviews to be preserved as part of a special project. *The Journal* did not survive without her; it was canceled by the end of the year she died.

After Barbara's funeral, as the procession of mourners drove to the cemetery, people stood at attention along the route, saluting. Her mother said Barbara would have been surprised by the warmth and love showered on her when she died. But the public understood what Barbara Frum had given them through her commitment to journalism and truth – what one friend called her "shining integrity." The outpouring and the salute were a tribute, and perhaps Barbara's greatest honor.

KATIE COURIC

"I didn't want to be this television sidekick who sort of giggled and did the features."

1957 -

Katie Couric once said being called cute made her "kind of puke." The same went for being described as perky. No journalist wants to be described that way; journalists are supposed to be serious professionals. Couric is an award-winning journalist who has made many historic breakthroughs, including being the first woman in the United States to be a solo nightly anchor on national television news. But, to do it, she had to overcome the image of herself as America's sweetheart – an image that helped bring her fame and fortune in the first place.

Katherine Ann Couric was born in Arlington, Virginia, on January 7, 1957. She was the youngest of John and Elinor

Couric's four children. Her father worked as a journalist and later in public relations. Her mother was a homemaker, and has been described as a feminist who taught her daughters to be strong and independent. All the Couric children were good students. Like her two sisters, Katie was a cheerleader in high school, and has been described by a friend from that time as an "all-American" kid who didn't get into trouble.

At university, Katie showed a strong interest in journalism, something that was encouraged by her father. She worked on the student newspaper and also volunteered at a radio station in the summer. Her father suggested she focus on broadcasting, and after graduation in 1979, she got her first news job at ABC television in Washington. It was a junior position, but it was a start. Eventually she moved to the all-news channel CNN, where she worked behind the scenes assigning stories. Her real goal was to be on air, and occasionally she got to do that. But when CNN's head of news saw her, he thought she looked too young, and said he never wanted to see her on air again.

Still, Katie persevered; she got a job as a reporter for a local network in Miami in 1984, and then in Washington in 1987. She did the kind of work every local reporter does, covering news of the city: immigration and crime stories in Florida, and everything from train crashes to politics in Washington. Politics was said to be her strength, but some people also noticed how natural she was on TV, and that she had a down-to-earth ability to tell stories about real people. She won her first Emmy, American television's top prize, for a story she did in Washington about a dating service for disabled people.

Reporting for local TV meant Katie was only seen on air in the city where she worked. But in 1989, she fulfilled the dream of many reporters by getting a national job that put her on air right across the country. NBC's Washington bureau chief hired her to cover the Pentagon – news from the Department of Defense. This was tough stuff; reporting on the military and its politics could be complicated, and some reporters called it the hardest beat in Washington. Katie later said it really helped elevate her reputation as a journalist, because "you can't be an airhead" and do stories about fighter jets.

It was a time of many good beginnings in Katie's life. She met Jay Monahan, a lawyer, in January 1989, and they married less than a year later. In 1990, NBC made her the first-ever national reporter for its morning show, called *Today*; this was in addition to her Pentagon job. That year, the network also sent Katie to Saudi Arabia, where U.S. troops were preparing for war with Iraq over its invasion of Kuwait. Katie did stories about the soldiers as well as the Saudi people. Covering war and conflict is considered a top assignment for reporters. Katie also demonstrated her news skills by helping break the story of exactly when the invasion would happen. Then, when a ceasefire was declared in February 1991, she was the first reporter to interview the leader of the U.S. Forces.

Katie's next step would launch her into a position where, as one NBC executive predicted, "everyone in America will know her name." In April 1991, NBC asked her to co-anchor the *Today* show. *Today* had been the leading U.S. morning news and talk show for many years, but the number of view-

> ### *Today, before Katie*
>
> In the early 1970s, Barbara Walters co-hosted the *Today* show with Frank McGee. McGee demanded Walters not be allowed to participate in serious interviews. Walters, who said her policy was "Work hard, don't whine," decided she had to fight back. NBC management finally said she could interview guests about serious subjects, but only after McGee asked the first three questions. Walters could then ask the fourth question.

ers had dropped, and program executives were looking for a way to bring them back. Katie, with her fresh, likeable on-air style, was their solution. The work was very different from reporting; it was in a studio, interviewing all sorts of guests, from politicians and newsmakers to celebrities. It was also one of the biggest jobs in TV. But Katie wasn't prepared to say yes right away.

Katie told NBC that she would only sign a contract if they agreed to give her the same number of "hard" news interviews as her male co-host, Bryant Gumbel. Hard news is the serious material – about important matters such as politics, major events, and disasters. Katie said that after being a journalist for eleven years, "I didn't want to be this television sidekick who sort of giggled and did the features." That's what happened to other female co-hosts. Before Katie Couric, one media analyst said, "the man did the hard news and sports, and the woman did the women's sphere – child rearing, clothes, and food. Katie smashed those stereotypes … She was the first modern woman on morning TV."

Katie took the job once NBC agreed to her conditions, and the news made national headlines. The network's belief that the thirty-four-year-old could bring back viewers was proven right. Ratings were going up. Both media critics and the audience recognized her ability to move easily from lighter subjects to more complex interviews. But it was her style that was making her a star. Some television critics raved. One wrote, "The hard part is finding a flaw … She's real, she's natural, she's totally at home on the air." Others noted her quick wit and easy smile. The downside of the media coverage was the constant reference to her being cute, or perky, which supported the image of her as a lightweight – someone who wasn't serious. Katie fought back, saying, "bunnies and ducks are perky." She also called it discriminatory, declaring, "I don't think men are described as perky."

Katie's critics had to take a step back when they saw what she did at the White House in October 1992. She was interviewing Barbara Bush, the wife of then-president George H. W. Bush, but as they were about to finish their live chat, the president himself dropped by. This was unheard of. Journalists often have to go through months of negotiations to get an interview with a president. But Bush went to Katie, live and on air, and allowed her to interview him for twenty minutes. She hadn't prepared for it, and had never interviewed president Bush before, but her work made national headlines, and she got glowing reviews. One television writer said she had shown once again "that she's worth her weight in gold." NBC apparently agreed. Prominent TV anchors are well paid, and in 1992 Katie reportedly signed a contract with the network for $1 million a year.

By the spring of 1997, Katie had helped bring viewer numbers for the *Today* show up to 10 million people. She and Jay had two daughters: Elinor, born in 1991, and Caroline, born in 1996. Their life was good, but chaotic. As a morning show host, Katie had to leave for the studio at 5 a.m. Jay had become a legal analyst with TV network MSNBC, which was also a demanding job. So when he started to feel achy and tired, he didn't immediately go to a doctor.

When Jay finally did get checked, he was diagnosed with colon cancer. Doctors operated, but the cancer had advanced too far. Less than a year after he was diagnosed, in January 1998, he died in hospital with Katie at his side. He was only forty-two years old. At forty-one, Katie was now a widow, with two young children aged six and two. Friends say Katie received more than 10,000 letters and cards from people all over the world after Jay's death. One month later, she went back on air, wearing her wedding ring on a chain around her neck. She told her audience she could not describe the devastation of the loss.

Katie was determined to try to help others avoid the same fate. The best way to cure colon cancer is to find it early, and that requires a test called a colonoscopy. A tube with a camera is put inside the bowel. Despite the test's embarrassing nature, Katie decided to have one done on herself on national TV. She wanted her audience to understand that it was not difficult or painful. This program was part of a special series she did on colon cancer; afterwards, the number of colonoscopies increased so dramatically that some people called it "the Couric effect." The programs won a prestigious Peabody Award, but more importantly to Katie, they would help save lives. She also started a cancer research foundation in Jay's name. But his death was not the end of Katie's losses. In 2001, her sister Emily, a U.S. senator, died of pancreatic cancer. Katie later confessed in an interview that she had never thought such terrible things would happen to her. "I had lived a charmed life and thought it would continue indefinitely," she said. "But the charm ran out."

In 2004, after thirteen years at the *Today* show, Katie set a new record in journalism when she signed a contract that reportedly paid her $65 million over four years, likely making her the highest-paid journalist in history – male or female. But this incredible success turned the tables on her popularity, at least with the media. Before this, she had been named "Hero of the Year" and one of America's most admired women. Now, gossip magazines attacked her, and she was criticized for being more of a celebrity than a journalist. Others pointed out that a man who made that much money wouldn't be condemned for it. But the criticism hurt her when she took her next historic step.

In the spring of 2006, CBS television announced that Katie was leaving NBC to become the first-ever solo female anchor of network news. She was also named Managing Editor of CBS news, and a contributor to the investigative program *60*

Minutes. Male news anchors had been the tradition for more than fifty years. Although two women had previously served as network news anchors, they had co-anchored with men, and the difficulties they'd experienced made those jobs short-lived. Many applauded Katie's appointment, saying it was about time. Others fiercely condemned it, saying she wasn't a serious enough journalist for the job. Her work on the *Today* show, interviewing entertainers and covering lighter events such as parades, came back to haunt her. Still, supporters sprang to her defence. The highly respected *New York Times* wrote about the hard news stories she had covered and how well she handled them. At NBC, Katie had reported on everything from presidential elections to the September 11th terrorist

Katie Couric at the 2004 Summer Olympics.

attacks and the tragic massacre at Columbine High School. Former news anchor Connie Chung said, "Katie has covered world news. She has covered breaking news. She has interviewed presidents, prime ministers, kings, and presidential candidates. She's a superb reporter and a superb anchor."

Katie made her debut on *CBS Evening News with Katie Couric* in September 2006. CBS had been last in TV news ratings for many years, and just like NBC fifteen years earlier, CBS executives hoped Katie would change that. She did, but only for a short time. Two years later, the network was back in last place. Perhaps for the first time in Katie's career, people were using the word "failure," and saying she might be fired. But the 2008 presidential election was coming up, and Katie excelled in politics. She covered the Democratic and Republican party conventions for CBS that summer, and national newspapers once again praised her work. Then came the interviews with vice-presidential candidate Sarah Palin.

Palin was governor of Alaska, and the announcement that she would run for vice president with Republican presidential candidate John McCain hit like a bombshell. Many voters,

First Female Co-Anchor, 1976

In 1976, Barbara Walters became the first female co-anchor on nightly national news in the U.S., with Harry Reasoner on ABC. Walters said Reasoner didn't want a partner and the country didn't want a woman reading the news. She left after two years and became one of television's most recognizable and successful people, doing high-profile interviews, winning top journalism awards, and eventually producing and hosting *The View*, a program she co-owns.

and many in the media, were taken with Palin's apparently straight-talking, fresh approach and were pleased to see a female candidate. It looked as though Palin was taking the wind out of the sails of Barack Obama's campaign for the Democrats. Then, in September, she was interviewed by Katie Couric.

If she were to be elected vice president, Palin would be second-in-command of the United States, and would become president should anything happen to John McCain. So Katie asked her tough and important questions about many aspects of the job, including the economy and world politics. Palin's answers revealed a lack of experience and knowledge, and were considered so embarrassing that many Republicans began to question whether she was a suitable candidate. *Newsweek* magazine asked, "Can we now admit the obvious? Sarah Palin is utterly unqualified to be vice-president." The popular comedy program *Saturday Night Live* spoofed Palin's interviews with Katie. The skits were seen by millions, both on television and the Internet, and were likely the final blow to McCain and Palin's campaign. Barack Obama won the election, becoming the first African-American president.

Many thought Katie Couric's interviews made the difference. She won at least two highly prestigious awards for

Second Female Co-Anchor; 1993

After Barbara Walters, it took sixteen years before a network debuted a woman in the co-anchor chair for weeknight national news again. In 1993, Connie Chung joined Dan Rather on CBS. Like Walters, she left after only two years, moving to ABC's newsmagazine program 20/20, and then to news channel MSNBC.

this work. In 2010, Columbia University's Graduate School of Journalism said that Katie's determined questions "prompted the most revealing remarks and had the greatest impact on the presidential campaign." They presented her with the distinguished Alfred I. duPont-Columbia University Award. She also won the Walter Cronkite Award for Excellence in Television Political Journalism, for what was called her "extraordinary" achievement. Katie has won many awards, including six Emmys, but – given the rumors that had swirled before the presidential campaign, predicting she was going to be fired – these two may have been the sweetest.

With her confidence renewed, Katie later joked about the rumors, borrowing a line from the famous American humorist Mark Twain. She said, "I think reports of my death were greatly exaggerated." She has expanded her news presence, moving to the Internet with a webcast show called *@katiecouric*. During her thirty years in news, Katie Couric has walked the line from success to near failure and back again. Her place in journalistic history is assured. And, certainly, no one is going to call her cute.

Two Solo Female News Anchors; 2009

In 2009, four years after Katie Couric's historic appointment, ABC announced it would also have a woman, Diane Sawyer, as its solo network news anchor. Two of the three major American network news programs now had solo female anchors. Connie Chung said it was gratifying the two women didn't have to share with men – something she and Walters had to do.

ANNA POLITKOVSKAYA

"In reporting this war, you have no right to think of yourself."

1958 - 2006

Great heroes are not always loved by their own people. In the case of Russian journalist Anna Politkovskaya, her heroism was not just in her actions, it was also in her words. But they were words her country and its leaders did not want to hear. Anna made it her mission to report the horrible cruelties of a Russian war she believed was unjust and had to be stopped. That mission cost Anna her life.

Anna could have lived an easier life than the one she chose. She was born into privileged circumstances compared to most Russians. Her parents, Stepan and Raisa Mazepa, were appointed by their government to work as diplomats at the United Nations in New York City. That's where Anna was born, on August 30, 1958. In the United States, Anna, her parents, and her older sister, Elena, had much more freedom than people had at home. In Russia, people's lives were strictly controlled: the government decided where they could live, where they could work, even what they could read. Many books were banned by the government because it did not agree with the ideas in them. In Anna's home, they had those banned books in their library. She loved reading and, by the time she was eleven, she was reading a book every day. Although Anna didn't like to talk about herself when she was older, she once told an interviewer that as a child, she was "a bit of a swot" – an expression for being a nerd.

In 1964, the Mazepa family returned to Moscow, the capital of Russia. Anna was a privileged child there as well, going to a special school reserved for the families of people in government. Russia was part of a vast system of states called the Union of Soviet Socialist Republics, ruled by the Communist Party. Under Communism, everyone was supposed to be equal, but in reality, people working for the government, such as Anna's parents, were much wealthier than the general public and enjoyed greater opportunities in life. The Mazepas, however, were said to be kind people. They had grown up in the Ukraine, a part of the Soviet Union that had experienced great hardships, including hunger and starvation. Their grandson, Anna's son,

Anna's Names

Anna's last name, Politkovskaya, was slightly different from her husband's, Politkovsky, because in Russia there are masculine and feminine versions of last names.

Anna's family name, Mazepa, is famous in Russia. Three centuries ago, Ivan Mazepa was a warrior who led a revolt against Russian czar Peter the Great over the control of his Ukrainian homeland. He lost the battle, thousands were killed, and he died in exile.

said they taught his mother "how to respond to people's troubles" and that "they never forgot the suffering they had seen."

Anna studied journalism at Moscow State University. She dated Alexander Politkovsky while she was there, and they married in 1978, before she graduated. Sasha, as he was known, was already working in journalism. They had two children soon after the marriage, a son, Ilya, and a daughter, Vera. But Anna continued her studies and graduated in 1980, the same year Vera was born. Anna's first job was part-time at a Moscow newspaper, *Izvestia*. She left there for a full-time job with the magazine for the Russian airline, Aeroflot. The work gave her free tickets to fly anywhere in the country, which Anna said was wonderful. "Thanks to this I saw the whole of our huge country. I was a girl from a diplomatic family, a reader …" she said. "I didn't know life at all."

All this must have made for a pleasant lifestyle. Anna had a good job, and Sasha was becoming one of Russia's best-known faces, hosting a television news show. Then, in the later 1980s, a massive historic change began in Russia under the new Communist Party leader, Mikhail Gorbachev. He introduced policies called *glasnost*, which means "openness." Journalists were thrilled, because this openness included the news media. Up to then, they had only

Propaganda and Censorship

In the former Soviet Union, the media was used for propaganda. Propaganda is untruthful, misleading, or dishonest information that is intentionally given to people to make them think in a certain way. For example, if a government wants to stay in power, it will give the public information that makes it look good, even if that information is not true. Withholding the truth, or preventing it from being told, is called censorship. Many organizations and countries use both propaganda and censorship.

been able to report what the government allowed, because it didn't want people to have any information that made the government look bad. In 1986, for example, there was an explosion at the Chernobyl nuclear plant in the Soviet Union. Poisonous gas escaped and began to float around the world, but the Soviet media did not report it. Under Gorbachev, things began to change.

Anna called the new freedom "a joy." She said, "It was simple happiness that you could read and think and write whatever you wanted." The previous restrictions must have been terrible for journalists. Anna began working for a newspaper again. In 1994, she started at *Obschchaya Gazeta*, one of the new independent papers. It was critical of the government, but with the new openness, this was allowed.

At *Obschchaya Gazeta*, Anna wrote about culture and did feature interview stories with known personalities. She was still part of a privileged minority; she and her husband, with his television fame, had enough money to send their son to private school in England, and Anna, who was a striking looking woman, was also known for dressing in high fashion.

Then she decided to do a story on refugee children from Chechnya. Chechnya was a republic almost completely surrounded by Russian territory. It had been ruled by Russia for more than one hundred years, but it wanted independence. In fact, because of the new openness, or *glasnost*, so many states had declared independence that the formerly powerful Soviet Union actually disbanded in 1991. But Russia kept control of Chechnya, which ignited a war. Desperate Chechen refugees fled to Moscow to seek help. Anna met these people in August 1996. It was a meeting that would profoundly change her life.

The refugees included children whose parents were dead, wives and husbands whose partners had been killed, and sick elderly people. The woman running the refugee center said that seeing the suffering of these people changed Anna. The elite woman in the beautiful clothes began helping the families, raising money, and doing whatever else she could. It was the start of Anna's relationship with Chechnya and its people.

Not long after this, the president of Russia signed a peace agreement with Chechnya. It did not grant independence but it did end the war. This was partly thanks to the news media, whose reports about the war's casualties had created a huge public outcry, forcing Russia to withdraw. For the first time, journalists had an impact on their country's actions. Anna had not covered the war, but she believed it was Russian journalism's finest triumph.

At the same time, Anna's home life had been falling apart. A close friend and co-worker of her husband's had been murdered, and her husband was having difficulties in his job. He began drinking heavily, there were terrible arguments, and by 1999, Sasha told Anna he wanted a divorce. That was the same year Anna changed jobs, becoming a reporter for *Novaya Gazeta*, another independent and democratic paper.

The 1990s had been a golden time for journalistic freedom in Russia, but that was coming to an end. By 1999, a man named Vladimir Putin was in power. Putin had been a part of a greatly feared spy agency. He was working on a plan to put Russian soldiers back in Chechnya when a series of explosions in Russian cities killed hundreds of people.

Russian authorities blamed Chechen terrorists. A reporter for *Novaya Gazeta* wrote there was evidence the authorities themselves may have planted the bombs in order to blame Chechens and gain support for a new war. But nobody paid attention to this. The Russian people were happy to support a renewed war, and in September 1999, what was called the Second Chechen War began. Now the government took greater control of the media, especially television, where most Russians get their news. Putin was taking the country back to the old ways of propaganda and censorship.

Anna was determined to report on the war, although her family was frantic with fear for her. She went to the Chechen city of Grozny, which was being bombed by Russian planes. Running with people trying to escape those bombs, she had to dive to the ground, which, she wrote, was starting to resemble "a deathbed." She also discovered more than one hundred elderly people who had been abandoned by staff in a nursing home, with no heat or water. She made a deal between the two warring sides so the patients could be taken out of the battle zone to safety.

This was the first of forty-eight trips Anna would make to Chechnya. One reporter said it was "one of the most dangerous stories in the world to cover." She witnessed rocket attacks that hit a market and maternity hospital, killing dozens of women and children. She reported on mass killings of villagers, rapes, torture, and kidnappings. She investigated what the Russian army was doing to its own soldiers, and said it was responsible for beatings that killed more than five hundred men. Besides writing for the newspaper, she also wrote several books that were translated into English and published abroad. The first was called *A Dirty War: A Russian Reporter in Chechnya*. A few years later, *A Small Corner of Hell: Dispatches from Chechnya* was published.

Anna believed the war was driven by racial hatred for the Chechens, who are mostly Muslim. She was deeply ashamed of what her country was doing and believed it was her duty to tell people what was happening. "One must always tell the truth. This was the principle she always lived by," her husband, Sasha, said. "And it was precisely what took her to Chechnya."

Reporting on Chechnya put Anna's life at risk, and not just because she sometimes worked in a war zone. In fact, Anna didn't call herself a war reporter; she said what she did was the "journalism of action." But Putin's government and Russian authorities despised her for what she wrote about them. Once, the Russian army imprisoned her, tortured her, and made her believe they would kill her. Another time, an officer threatened her life after she reported that he was involved in a case of torture. And on a flight to help in a hostage-taking by Chechens, she was poisoned and nearly died. The Russian authorities didn't want her there. Anna had tried to negotiate with Chechen terrorists in another hostage taking in a Moscow theater in 2002. But the Russian forces pumped poison gas into the building, and more than one hundred hostages, and many of the Chechens, died.

Anna reported abuses on both sides of the war, and was critical of both. Her newspaper was one of the few where Chechnya was written about openly, but it didn't have a wide readership. And, to make sure Anna's influence was not too broad, the government banned her from Russian TV. But Anna wrote that Russians did not want to hear what she had to say anyway. She believed it was because Putin had improved the economy, and they didn't want their comfortable lives disturbed by upsetting news.

Still, the Russian Union of Journalists recognized her

Following Her Conscience

Anna was interviewed for a documentary, called *Democracy on Deadline*, about reporters who take great risks to do their work. "Everyone has a conscience," she said. "I think that I currently fulfill all the obligations I have to my conscience. Everyone else must do it too. Pushing aside information about what is happening near you in your time is shameless."

work and gave Anna its Golden Pen Award. Outside Russia, her books drew attention to the war and to Anna's bravery in reporting it. She received many international awards, including Amnesty International's Global Award for Human Rights Journalism, the Prize for Journalism and Democracy from the Organization for Security and Cooperation in Europe, and the Olof Palme Prize for her brave and influential work in "the long battle for human rights in Russia."

But awards do not protect anyone, and any journalist critical of Putin was at risk. Two other reporters who worked with Anna at *Novaya Gazeta* died mysteriously – one apparently from being poisoned. A magazine reporter writing about Russia and Chechnya was gunned down and killed. Anna's sister, Elena Kudimova, said, "We all begged her to stop … My parents. Her editors. Her children. But she always answered the same way: 'How could I live with myself if I didn't write the truth?'"

Anna knew she could be killed. But in many interviews over the years, she kept repeating that the war – and Putin – were cruel and unjust. She hated Putin "for his racism, for his lies." In an American television interview, she said, "In reporting this war, you have no right to think of yourself." Getting the information out about Chechnya, "… that is worth a life." Even her own life.

But her work was taking a toll on her. Anna had always been a strong personality. Those who worked with her said she "was not an easy person." Her mission for justice in Chechnya consumed her, and sometimes this meant she was insulting even to friends and people trying to help her. She wasn't eating or sleeping properly. The head of her newspaper said, "… she used to be full of laughter and good humor. But the laughter diminished with every passing year."

Saturday October 7, 2006, was a busy day for Anna, who was at home in Moscow. The previous two weeks had been

A demonstation in memory of Anna Politkovskaya in Moscow, Russia, 2008.

very difficult. Her father had died of a heart attack and her mother was in hospital, diagnosed with cancer. Anna's daughter, Vera, was expecting a baby and had just moved in with her. That Saturday, Anna went grocery shopping, then parked outside her apartment building to take the groceries up. She delivered one load to her seventh-floor home, then went back to the lobby. A man was waiting for her there. He shot her four times, in a way that signalled it was a contract killing; somebody had hired the murderer to do the job. Anna was forty-eight years old.

October 7th is Vladimir Putin's birthday. Outside Russia, reports of Anna's death suggested the murder was a "gift" to Putin. A few days later, Putin spoke to foreign reporters and dismissed Anna's influence in Russia, saying it "was very minimal." Three men eventually stood trial for arranging the murder. They were found not guilty in 2009.

Despite Putin's dismissal of Anna's importance, hundreds lined up in the rain at her funeral. They wanted to honor the woman who put the obligation to tell the truth about suffering and injustice before all else. The president of the Russian organization to protect journalistic freedoms, the Glasnost Defense Foundation, said, "She had the facts and the truth, and for that she will always be a hero of Russia."

Murdered Russian Journalists

Between March 2000 and August 2009, twenty journalists were murdered or died under mysterious circumstances in Russia. Of these, five people, including Anna, worked at *Novaya Gazeta*. The Committee to Protect Journalists called it the third most dangerous place in the world for journalists.

PAM OLIVER

"I still get butterflies when they kick that ball."

1961 –

American football has been called a collision sport. Players run into one another at high speeds, tackle each other, and pull each other down. It's all part of the game, and Pam Oliver loves it. And sports fans love her. Pam has been called one of the top three female sportscasters in the United States. Others say her work as a football sideline reporter is simply, "the best." A popular American magazine called Pam "über-tough," as a compliment to her journalism. "Über" means "extremely," and this super-tough woman is willing to tackle anything or anyone in order to do her job.

It's never been easy to be a female sports journalist. The work has been almost entirely dominated by men, many of whom did not make women feel welcome. Women began to have a stronger presence in sports reporting in the 1970s, but they are still a small minority. In 2005, an expert estimated that women made up only ten percent of people in sports media. Many leave the industry because of harassment and discrimination. Some, like Pam Oliver, tough it out. She's been a sports reporter for nearly twenty years and says she has never considered giving it up.

Pam learned her love of football from her mother, Mary, who was "the biggest fan in the house" when they all gathered in front of the television for Sunday football. Her father, John, was in the military police with the U.S. Air Force. Pam was born in Dallas, Texas, on March 10, 1961, the youngest of three girls. As a military family, the Olivers moved every two to three years, and lived in at least five different states while Pam was growing up. Pam says it was hard to give up friends and start all over in a new place time after time. There was also conflict between her father and mother because Mary was a homemaker who wanted to work outside the house. Her parents split up and got back together more than once when Pam was young. Despite all this, Pam says her childhood living on military bases was a "great, solid, safe life."

Besides football, Pam also watched television news as a child and says she was a "news junkie" by the age of three. She would be glued to the TV, watching reporters do stories, while her mother was cooking dinner. Pam was fascinated by the people on the scene of an event,and liked to walk around the house, using a hairbrush as a microphone, pretending she was a reporter, too.

In elementary school, Pam's entered three races in a track meet and won them all. Her interest in athletics blossomed. She continued to be "deep, deep, deep" into sports as a teenager. Her parents finally divorced when she was fifteen, and Pam stayed with her dad so she could finish high school in

Niceville, Florida, near the Eglin Air Force Base where they lived. She was involved in track, and played basketball and tennis. But as one of only a handful of black people in her classes, she says she "just wanted out" of high school.

Pam wanted to study journalism at college, and she had her pick of schools when a number of them selected her for her athletic abilities. Pam chose a well known school for African-Americans, Florida Agricultural and Mechanical University, because she said she hadn't had the experience of being with black people, and it was something she needed. FAMU gave her a sports scholarship and – just as importantly – it had a strong journalism program.

Pam says her start there was the "most confusing year of my young life." She says her roommate was a lifesaver, helping her understand why she was having problems. "Girl," she would say to Pam, "you are such a white girl." Pam didn't fit in because she had grown up mostly in white culture, on the military bases and at school. Her roommate explained that the way Pam spoke and dressed, even the way she wore her belt, made her different from other students. Pam says some students wouldn't even speak to her, because they thought she was stuck up.

After her first year, she decided not to worry about being accepted. She had "never been someone to go home and cry because someone has been mean to me." She had friends on her track team and was a successful runner, setting a record for the 400-meter race that stood for at least twenty years. Her relay team won the university's first national track championship, and Pam also qualified for the Olympic trials, giving her a chance to compete in the world's top amateur athletic games. But she decided against it. By the time she graduated in 1984, she'd had enough of track. During school, she'd done some football reporting for the *Orlando Sentinel* newspaper and knew she wanted to be a reporter.

Groundbreaking Sportswriter

Mary Garber was one of the very few women writing about sports in the 1940s. She was banned from the press boxes, where male reporters worked, because she was female. Garber worked for North Carolina newspapers and covered every sport, including games at African-American colleges that were excluded from mainstream media. She continued writing after her retirement at age seventy and, in 2005, became the first woman to win the Associated Press Sports Editor award for her contribution to sports journalism.

During the next eight years, Pam moved around the country just as she had as a child, working as a TV reporter in Georgia, New York, Texas, and Florida. She covered everything from agriculture to space and science, as well as general news. But she always had her eye on the sports department. In Florida, she finally convinced a producer to hire her for sports, although he warned her that it would be career suicide – reporting sports was seen as a step down from news. Pam didn't care. Just one month later, ESPN, the biggest all-sports cable network in the world, called and offered her a job.

Unbelievably, she said no! She didn't think she had enough experience, so she took a sports job in Houston instead, to polish her skills. ESPN waited and, one year later, in 1993, hired her as a football and basketball reporter. Pam stayed at ESPN for two years. Then, in 1995, another large cable channel, FOX Sports, hired her.

At FOX, Pam worked as an anchor, but she became best known for her work as a sideline reporter covering the National Football League. NFL football is TV's most popular sport, and sideline reporters are down beside the field during a game, where all the action is. They interview the players, report on developments that may affect the game, and sometimes give their opinion on the play. Some people call them "sideline snoops" because they try to dig out information that players and coaches may not want the public to know. One time, information Pam revealed also ended up exposing the kind of discrimination female sports reporters face.

Pam reported that a player had a shouting match with an assistant coach. The player was embarrassed by this, and denied it. He also said that he was so angry he wanted to find Pam and "spank her with a ruler really, really hard." He said that he had once supported the idea of female reporters, but not if "they can't get their story straight." These remarks were considered so insulting they made national headlines. Pam stuck to her guns, saying, "My job is to report what I see. I do not make stories up."

Pam says no environment that is mostly male is going to be easy for a woman to enter. She also once said she had experienced more difficulties in her job from being a woman than from being African-American. Harassment and discrimination are always present, and a brief glance at comments about

"A Woman Has No Business"

In 2002, nationally known commentator Andy Rooney, ignoring the skills of Pam Oliver and others, said on a television sports show that "... those damn women down on the sidelines ... don't know what the hell they're talking about ... a woman has no business being down there trying to make some comment about a football game." Public reaction was mostly negative, but the comment demonstrated what some people still thought of women in sports media.

Pam says to do her job well, she has to think like an athlete.

female sports reporters on the Internet proves this. Many men rate them in terms of their attractiveness rather than their skills. Pam finds this "horrifying." Women have also had terrible experiences going into players' locker rooms after games. This is an essential part of the job, because it is often the only time and place to get players' comments. At one time, female reporters were banned from locker rooms. Then, in 1977, a woman reporter with *Sports Illustrated* sued, together with the magazine, to be allowed in. She won, but the legal victory did not stop women from being insulted and attacked. One female reporter received a live rat from a player after her locker room visit; another had ice water dumped on her. Many more were subject to nasty sexual put-downs.

Pam's job no longer includes going to locker rooms, for which she is grateful. She says the experience is "gross." But she has still experienced discrimination. Some people have assumed she is a cheerleader when they see her studying her football notes on a plane. She says other people think that because she's a woman and hasn't played football herself, "there's nothing you can tell them about the game." In the past, she has sometimes been excluded from important work meetings, or had what she thought was her assignment given to a man.

In spite of the difficulties, Pam says her enthusiasm for her job doesn't flag. "I still get butterflies when they kick that ball." In addition to her

Good Research = Good Reporting

Pam creates weekly notes for the games, covering each team's overall record, strengths and weaknesses of offense and defense, and player injuries. She also watches films of the teams' previous games. For player interviews, she says, "You have to really work to find something beyond the obvious ... I'm not comfortable if I haven't read every clip, every bio [biography] ... You don't want to get caught out there."

sideline work, she does feature stories that are more in-depth, about the game or the players. In a typical week, she will start on Monday and spend about three days researching material for upcoming games and reports. By Thursday, she travels to the game location, and begins shooting her feature. Friday and Saturday are spent on meetings, research, and writing. On Sunday, she arrives at the game site three hours in advance, talking to players and coaches. Then the game starts, and she's on air. The next day, it starts all over again.

Pam says her background as an athlete helps in her work. She knows what's involved in training and preparing in order to be the best. "I was athletic my whole life," she says. "To me, this job is a natural extension of what I've always been interested in."

Sideline reporters have to know the game and the athletes, inside out, and they sometimes have to be aggressive to get their material. Pam says her boss has called her "the pit bull," because of her aggressive style. "I ask the hard questions," she explains. While some people regard players as celebrities, Pam says you can't be "goo-goo" over them. So she's not at all shy about asking players things they may not want to talk about, or reporting things they say, but later wish they hadn't. Sometimes, this gets her in trouble.

Pam once reported that a quarterback told her in an interview he was unhappy on his team. Afterwards, the quarterback denied it. Pam was angry. She said he was calling her a liar, and from that point on she was "done with him." It took two years before she and the player eventually made peace. This was the incident for which the magazine GQ called her "über-tough." Pam says she is not afraid of conflict, and, like any good reporter, is "not in the business of being liked." Her readiness to stand up for herself has won her the admiration of many young women who want to be sports reporters.

For the most part, Pam says her experiences with athletes

have been overwhelmingly positive. They respect her, and many praise her hard work and professionalism. Other journalists do as well. In 2004, *Ebony*, one of the top magazines for African-Americans, honored her with an Outstanding Woman in Journalism award. Many articles noted her success in a world that is not only mostly male, but also mostly white. Pam has been a regular on Super Bowl games, which are the absolute peak of the football season, seen around the world in more than two hundred countries by hundreds of millions of people.

In 2004, Pam married another sports journalist, Alvin Whitney, whom she met on a blind date. Dating people who weren't in the sports world didn't work for her, she says, because they couldn't understand the lifestyle of constant work and travel. With her military upbringing, she says "it's not normal" for her to stay in one place. Pam says Alvin is her perfect match. He works covering the National Basketball Association, which Pam does as well, during the one month a year when she's not doing football. Pam keeps active, playing tennis with her husband, but she can't run any more because of her knees and back.

Groundbreaking Sportscaster

Lesley Visser was the first woman assigned to Monday Night Football and also the first assigned to a Super Bowl sideline. In 2006, she became the first woman to be recognized by the Pro Football Hall of Fame. Her work as a pioneer sports journalist was also recognized by the International Olympic Committee, which made her the first woman sportscaster to carry the Olympic Torch, in 2004.

Pam also takes time to help others, counseling younger female reporters and occasionally returning to her old journalism school to work with students. Young women, however, still have many barriers to break through. Some trends in TV sports are particularly disturbing. Television executives, in the hopes of increasing their male audience, sometimes hire women for the way they look rather than for their knowledge. Pam believes that strategy will eventually fail, because true sports lovers want expertise and good journalism.

Many media commentators have also noted, that as of January 2009, there is still is no permanent female play-by-play announcer in a broadcast booth. Play-by-play is often considered the top job in NFL television coverage. In fact, television networks rarely use women on a regular basis in the booth for any popular professional sport.

Pam has no ambition to be in the broadcast booth. For her, sideline reporting is "the cool part," being where everything happens, just as she imagined when she was a girl. She has conquered many of the prejudices facing women sports journalists, including one of the most persistent. As the media sports columnist of the large daily newspaper *USA Today* wrote, women "have had to fight the impression by the largely male viewerships wondering if they know their sports." Pam Oliver, he concluded, "knows her sports."

There is no bigger compliment than that.

FARIDA NEKZAD

"Afghan women's voices should be heard."

1976 -

When she was just twenty years old, Farida Nekzad left Afghanistan, vowing she would never return. A new and cruel group had taken power, one that posed great danger to her and her family. Five years later, that group, called the Taliban, was overthrown. So Farida broke her vow and returned home, hopeful that as a young journalist, she could help her people – especially women, who were treated so horribly under Taliban rule. Despite threats to her life, renewed war in her country, and the murder of other female journalists, she has since promised never to leave Afghanistan again. She believes it is the duty of people like her to stay, and that it is the only way to ensure women's voices will be heard and their lives improved. "We can bring change by our staying," she says. "I stay because of the future, because of my country, because of women."

Farida's country has a long and sad history of war, and of restrictions on women's freedoms. In the past and into the 1950s, women were not allowed to show their faces in public and had to hide themselves by wearing veils. There was also a practice called purdah, which kept women separate from men, and sometimes meant women were almost entirely confined to their houses. Often, girls were not allowed to attend schools. But when Farida was born in the capital city of Kabul on November 1,1976, it seemed girls in Afghanistan would have more opportunities. The country's new president was in the process of increasing women's rights, and many changes had been made, including allowing women to attend university.

Like most Afghans, Farida's family was Muslim, following the religion of Islam. Her parents, Mashkokan and Najiba, had ten children: four boys and six girls. Farida's early childhood was a relatively peaceful time. But just after her third birthday, a powerful country called the Soviet Union invaded Afghanistan and a ten-year war began. Life in Kabul became very dangerous. Farida says the terrible fighting took away "all of our happiness during childhood." Her family was also in danger because Farida and her sisters went to school. Her father was threatened by people who didn't believe he should let his daughters be educated. This is probably one of the reasons why, even as a young child, Farida hoped to do something to change the lives of women in her country.

She became interested in journalism when she was a teenager. A female neighbor in Kabul was a reporter for the *Kabul Times* newspaper. Farida went to her house every night to learn English, and the neighbor encouraged her to try journalism as a career. During high school, Farida worked on school newspapers and, in the early 1990s, entered Kabul

University to study journalism. By this time, the Soviets had been defeated, but life remained difficult and dangerous. Now there were battles between different Afghan groups over who would rule the country. Once, because of the continued fighting, Farida and her family left Afghanistan for eight months. When they came back, their home had been looted, and they had lost many of their belongings.

In 1996, the Taliban won power. They made new laws that they said would create a more religious way of life. Many believed these laws had nothing to do with following Islam or being a good Muslim. But the Taliban severely punished anyone who did not agree with them. People were tortured and executed in public, as a way of showing what would happen if you disobeyed. Some people disappeared and were never

When the Taliban came to power in 1996, women were forced to wear burkas so their faces and bodies were hidden when they were in public.

heard from again. Women's rights were immediately taken away. Returning to some of the old ways, the Taliban said women had to stay inside their homes, and could not work. Girls' schools were closed. If women did have to go out, they had to be completely covered by a large, loose piece of clothing called a burka that went over their heads and right down to their toes with just a small, veiled rectangular opening for their eyes. The Taliban were brutal. Sometimes, if a Taliban man saw a woman in the street whom he thought wasn't dressed properly, he would whip her. There were many other laws: no music, movies, television, or even kite flying which had been a favorite Afghan pastime.

Farida's family soon decided they could not live with the terror of Taliban rule. Farida, together with an older brother and two younger sisters, were the first in the family to flee across the border to Pakistan, in 1996. Her father feared that Farida was in the most danger, because at school she had done some work for a foreign organization, and the Taliban hated most things that were foreign. She had to quit university, and says she will never forget the day she left. Even now, she finds it painful to think about. Farida cried all the way from Kabul to the Pakistan border because she felt so hopeless and sad about leaving her studies. The rest of her family followed a few months later. During the next few years, Farida taught in schools in Pakistan and worked with Afghan refugees.

In September 2001, terrorists used passenger airplanes to attack New York City's World Trade Center and other sites in the United States. About 3,000 people were killed, and around the world there was horror at the loss of innocent lives. The terrorists were part of a group that had been supported by the Taliban, and they were believed to be hiding in Afghanistan. The United States and Great Britain joined forces and began a war in Afghanistan in October 2001. By the first week of December, the Taliban had been defeated. Their strict laws were thrown out. Women were once again allowed to work outside the home, go to school, and – at least in the cities – were not forced to wear the burka. Although conditions in much of the country were desperate after years of Taliban rule and previous wars, many people were now hopeful for the future.

Farida was still in Pakistan. She says she could not believe the Taliban had been defeated, "because they were very strong and cruel." But seeing the changes happening in the country, she and her family returned home in 2002. Many parts of Kabul had been ruined. Still, the restored freedoms for women, Farida said, were uplifting. "It was a great strength for me."

Farida wanted to work as a journalist, so she could support women gaining their rights and report about their lives. There was an important reason why women had to be journalists. In many parts of Afghan society, men and women are still separated, and men are often not allowed to be in certain places with women. "Men do not have access to women suffering in hospitals, homes, schools, and workplaces," Farida said. "So if women do not write about them, who would?" Women were needed as reporters, because they were often the only ones allowed to talk to women. Without female journalists, stories of half of Afghan society – the women – could not be told.

After the Taliban, there were many breakthroughs for women journalists. A female radio announcer who had previously been banished was actually the first voice on Radio Afghanistan to announce that Kabul had been liberated. A women's magazine had started up, as well as a radio station. Farida, now in her mid-twenties, began her work as a journalist by writing about individual people and their lives. She told the story of a woman who started a beauty salon, for example, which would have been of great interest to Afghan women. They had been forbidden the use of beauty items, even nail polish, under the Taliban. Farida also worked as a radio reporter and a talk show host. She reported on women's rights, but also on the daily news – everything from accidents to dishonest leaders. Sometimes she went outside Kabul to the rural areas for her work. This was a brave and unusual step, since people there were less open in their views of women, often still requiring them to wear the burka.

People from other countries went to Afghanistan to support and train journalists. Jane McElhone, a Canadian radio producer working for an international organization founded in Canada, was one of them. Jane and other trainers taught dozens of Afghan women to be reporters. Afghanistan was now

Farida Nekzad oversaw other journalists at Pajhwok News, and became one of the few Afghan women in media management.

a democracy, so these women reporters would, for example, tell the audience how elections worked and about the importance of voting. Afghans, who had been cut off from the world by the Taliban, needed journalists to provide them with as much information as possible.

In 2003, Jane hired Farida to do radio reports about women and life after the war. She worked on one story at this time that resulted in a death threat. It was about Afghanistan's warlords: men who have their own independent armies and who battle for their own private powers. One day when Farida got into a taxicab, the driver started yelling at her, saying he knew she was a journalist who wrote about the warlords. "You're going to be killed," he said. "You're a woman, you should just go home and stay there." Farida asked him to stop the car, but he wouldn't. When he slowed down to go around a corner, she jumped out while the car was still moving. She was injured – her hand and arm were cut and bleeding – but she was alive.

It was frightening, but it didn't stop Farida from continuing her work. In fact, by 2004, she had moved to an even higher-ranking job. She helped create a news agency called Pajhwok News. Pajhwok means "echo." It employed many reporters, telling news stories every day in the two official languages of Afghanistan, Dari and Pashto, as well as in English. Farida became its top manager – the editor-in-chief – and one of the few women in Afghanistan in a top media position. The stories Pajhwok covered were sometimes controversial. One was about a warlord who traded his dog for a young girl. Farida said that people working for the warlord threatened the reporter after the story aired, saying, "Apologize. Otherwise we will kill you."

Farida had been head of Pajhwok for about a year when the Taliban began launching attacks again. It became clear that the war against them had not been completely won. The risk of being a journalist in Afghanistan increased with the

Afghan Media Women Murdered 2005-2007

May 2005 Shaima Rezayee, 24.
Idol to young Afghan people because of her popular television program about music. She was fired after being criticized for her program's style, which some religious people called immoral. Three months later, she was shot and killed in her home.

May 2007 Shekaiba Sanga Amaaj, 22.
A television news presenter in Kabul. Murdered in her home.

June 2007 Zakia Zaki, 35.
Director of a radio station whose name in English means "Peace Now." Shot and killed in her home, in front of her son.

escalating conflicts. And, since one of the Taliban's goals was to end women's freedoms, female journalists were especially at risk. The warlords also continued to threaten them. In 2005, the murder of Afghan media women began, with the shooting of a former TV music show host, Shaima Rezayee. Exactly who is responsible and the reasons for this murder – and others – are unknown. Some say the murders were done by family members, some blame the warlords. Others say the women were targeted because they worked for media that received help from foreign organizations. Or that they were killed because they had jobs outside the home. Whatever the reasons, many think the murderers will never be found.

Farida had known Zakia Zaki for five years, and had visited her radio station, before Zaki was murdered in 2007. Zaki had publicly criticized the warlords. The death of her media colleague and friend brought new threats to Farida. After attending the funeral, she got a message on her cell phone saying that she too would be killed – "just like Zakia." Despite this and the fear created by the murders, Farida and others like her did not waver in their commitment to journalism.

In October 2007, shortly before her thirty-first birthday,

Farida married. Her husband, Rahimullah Samander, is also a journalist. She says that her husband, her husband's family, and her own family – especially her "great father" – all support her in what she does. But they also worry about her. If someone planned to kill her, they would likely follow her daily routine to see how and where they could most easily attack. So Farida tries to ensure that nothing about her day is predictable. She takes different cars on different routes to work, and even sleeps in different rooms of her house. But living like this is stressful and difficult. Farida says, "Every day I leave home, I am not sure if I will return." She also says, however, "Whether I am dead or alive, the struggle should continue. Afghan women's voices should be heard." The courage of Farida and other Afghan women journalists is recognized by people around the world. Shortly after her wedding, Farida traveled to Toronto to receive the International Press Freedom Award from the organization called Canadian Journalists for Free Expression. She said the award was an honor for all Afghan women. "It gives the message we are not alone. This kind of award gives us the power to work harder."

When she was in New York the following year to accept another journalism award for her courage, Farida had some wonderful personal news. She was pregnant. And, she said,

Working Together

In an interview in 2008 in Canada, Farida Nekzad spoke about her impressions of Toronto. "In Toronto I see in one building many people work from different countries and different languages, and they are ... very friendly, no conflicts." She said she wished she could see that in Afghanistan as well.

she hoped the baby was a girl. She wanted a daughter who would one day have the freedom of speech that so many Afghan women have not had over the centuries, and still have to fight for today.

In May 2009, Farida got her wish. She and her husband gave their baby girl a beautiful name: Muska. The name means "smile."

THEMBI NGUBANE

" ... just talking about this has the power to change lives."

1985 - 2009

Thembi Ngubane had a beautiful voice. Like her name, it was wonderfully African. Her voice flowed and lilted and swam around words, especially words with "r" in them. She rolled the r's around her tongue as if they were a song. And her song was a prayer, one she spoke each morning as she began the day. "Hello," she would say to the mirror. But she was not speaking to herself. She was speaking to the illness in her body, a virus called HIV. She wanted to tell the virus that she, Thembi, was the boss of her body – not the disease. "Hello, HIV, you trespasser," she said, rolling those r's. "You are in my body. You have to obey the rules. You have to respect me."

Thembi Ngubane was from South Africa, and like more than five million others in her country, she had the virus that causes the illness called AIDS. But in South Africa, despite the number of people who suffer from AIDS, it is considered a terribly shameful disease to have. Fearing how they might be treated, those who are sick try to keep it secret. Thembi decided not to do that. She reported the story of her illness on radio, a story that would eventually be heard by millions around the world. She did it because she wanted to help prevent other young people from getting sick, and she wanted people to stop feeling ashamed.

Thembi was born April 19, 1985. She was raised for most of her childhood by her mother, outside the city of Cape Town in Khayelitsha, a huge sprawling township of more than two million people. It is a poor place – sometimes called a shanty-town because many of the homes there are shacks, made only of wood, tar paper, and tin. Later in her life, when Thembi had a chance to travel, she said she came to realize that being poor in Khayelitsha was not so bad. "I pitied myself that I lived in a poor community," she wrote. "But I see that even if I lived in a shack, I still had a bed to sleep on and food to eat."

Thembi's mother, Nosizwe, spoke Zulu; her father, Mbambeleli, who lived in a different part of the country, spoke Xhosa. Thembi spoke both of these South African languages, and also learned English in school.

Thembi was in high school when she found out she had the HIV virus that causes AIDS. AIDS attacks the body's immune system, and often results in death. Thembi didn't feel sick, but a former boyfriend had died, and no one would tell her why. She was worried it was because of AIDS, and frightened she might have it, too. One of the most common ways to get AIDS is by having sex with someone who is infected. She decided to get tested, and said the news that she did indeed have the virus "was like an earthquake." Even though she felt and looked perfectly normal, she thought everyone could see that she had it. She was not only afraid she might die; she was also afraid of people's reactions, because having AIDS was such a terrible stigma in South Africa. Some women with AIDS were thrown out of their homes and abandoned by their families. In Thembi's township, people sometimes burned down the houses of those who were sick. Just a few years before Thembi was diagnosed, a young South African woman decided she would tell people she had AIDS, because she wanted to help stop discrimination. She was found beaten to death. No one was ever charged with the murder.

Although she was only sixteen years old and had not finished her education, Thembi quit school after her diagnosis. She got work as a hairdresser, and began to do volunteer work, including putting up posters persuading people to get tested for AIDS. She still kept her illness secret, but met with a group of other people who had AIDS; they were able to talk openly and support one another. Thembi was also part of a youth organization, and that's where she met an American radio producer named Joe Richman. Joe created programs for the U.S. National Public Radio network, or NPR. He asked Thembi if she would be interested in tape recording her experiences as a young woman living with AIDS. It

AIDS in South Africa

In 2008, UNAIDS, the joint United Nations program on HIV and AIDS, released its latest numbers. It estimated that in South Africa:

At least 18 per cent of all people, or as many as one in five, had HIV. This is one of the highest rates of HIV infection in the world.

5,700,000 adults and children were living with HIV.

3,200,000 women over fifteen years of age were living with HIV.

would be a form of diary, but one that she would speak instead of write, and it would run on the radio. Joe would give her a microphone and tape recorder, and she would record her daily life, thoughts, and conversations. She agreed, because the diary was only going to play in the United States, in English; people in South Africa would not hear it, and her AIDS would still be a secret there.

Thembi was amused when she got the tape recorder. "I was excited," she said, "thinking I was going to get ... a fancy, smart, sexy tape recorder, only to find out he just gave me a huge, ugly black old tape recorder with a huge mike and huge earphones. Imagine carrying that ... around Khayelitsha, everyone thinking I was going crazy!" After she had it, Thembi talked to her boyfriend, Melikhaya Mpumela, on tape. Melikhaya was the first person she told about her diagnosis in 2002, because she was afraid if she was sick, then he was in danger of getting the disease. At first he didn't believe her because she looked so healthy. Then he became frightened and told his family. They didn't know much about AIDS and made the two break up. Before long, though, Thembi and Melikhaya got back together, and he got tested. The results showed he also had the virus. Melikhaya said he didn't blame Thembi, and the two of them decided to educate their families about the illness. Eventually, Thembi said, both their families became supportive.

For more than a year, in 2004 and 2005, Thembi recorded her experiences and thoughts. She said talking into the microphone helped her. "I was ... just pouring my heart into it and what I really liked was that the diary was not talking back. The diary was not judging me. It was just there when I needed it." She also taped a trip to the doctor and a conversation with her mother. Thembi then went to visit her father to record a difficult thing: telling him she had AIDS. She had not been able to bring herself to tell him for the three years since she had been diagnosed. Afterwards, she said it was "one of the hardest things" she had ever done. But her father told her, "What can I do? I have to accept it … OK, my kid."

Thembi also told people on tape about a surprise she had for them. She and Melikhaya had a baby! Having a baby can be risky for someone with AIDS, because the woman might pass on the disease to the infant through her body before birth. But Thembi really wanted to be a mother and, as she told her own mother, "I felt like I needed something to live for." She talked to her doctor, and he helped and supported her. Melikhaya and Thembi's daughter, Onwabo, was born in November 2004; the baby tested negative for AIDS.

In January 2005, Thembi stopped recording her diary for a few months when she became very sick. She didn't want to go to hospital, because she was still afraid of what people would think of her, but her mother took her there. That's where Thembi changed her mind about keeping the story of her illness secret in South Africa. Surrounded by other AIDS patients, she said she could see it was not just the disease that was killing them. Thembi believed they were also dying because they were ashamed, and because of that shame, they weren't able to tell people about their sickness. "It was then I thought, how can I be doing this for the U.S. and not for South Africa?" she said. "It is in South Africa that people need to hear this." She decided speaking out was something she could do to help her country. Her story could reach and teach others.

Thembi got better, and also became one of the lucky few, who, because of the volunteer group Doctors Without Borders, was given special drugs that help fight AIDS. With her new decision to be open about her illness, she went on speaking tours in South Africa. Joe Richman says this gave them the idea that Thembi should also do a speaking tour in the United States when her diary went to air. He said that when she spoke she was so confident and beautiful, and such a good speaker, audiences were shocked when she told them, "I have AIDS."

Joe Richman took about fifty hours of recordings from Thembi and edited them into a twenty-three-minute documentary. On Thembi's twenty-first birthday, in April 2006, NPR aired the diary for the first time. Thembi, Melikhaya, and Joe were together in the United States for the broadcast. Although Thembi had no education as a journalist, she had now become a reporter – a reporter, as Joe called her, "of her own life." This is sometimes called personal journalism, because people tell their own stories. It has become an increasingly popular form of reporting.

The response to Thembi was overwhelming. She toured five cities: New York, Chicago, Boston, Washington, and Los Angeles. She spoke to people in schools, churches, and even to a packed auditorium of Hollywood celebrities. In Washington, Thembi met with members of Congress. In New York, she made a television appearance on CNN – alongside former U.S. president Bill Clinton – as part of a panel discussion on AIDS.

In March 2007, Thembi's diary aired in her own country – in Xhosa, Zulu, and English. She went on tour in South Africa again, to speak once more about discrimination. She also desperately wanted to convince young people, especially young women, to take precautions if they had sex, so they would not get the illness as she had. She wrote that sometimes when she looked out at the girls in the audience, she thought of her daughter, Onwabo, and it gave her strength. She believed "just talking about this has the power to change lives." Melikhaya was often with her when she spoke, and sometimes women asked him how it felt to be with the woman who infected him. He replied that it was an honor.

One of the most significant parts of her tour was when she spoke to the country's Parliament. South Africa's government had been severely criticized for ignoring the AIDS epidemic devastating the country, for allowing continued discrimination against people with AIDS, and for sometimes saying there wasn't a problem at all. When Thembi spoke to the politicians, she urged them to accept that "AIDS is here."

The radio diary played all over the English-speaking world. It was translated into French for French-speaking African countries, and into Spanish for Mexico. Because it played on the British service called BBC World, Joe estimates that on radio alone, Thembi's diary has reached at least 50 million

You can hear Thembi Ngubane's diary and see more photographs online at http://www.aidsdiary.org/story.html.

You can also read her blog about her tour of South Africa at http://thembisaidsdiarytour.vox.com.

people. It also won an Overseas Press Club award for best international radio story of 2006.

But people did not need a radio to hear Thembi. Millions more could hear her and watch videos of her on the Internet. That's where Thembi ventured into another form of journalism: the blog. She wrote and posted frequent reports about her South African tour on a website, increasing the numbers she was able to reach with her message.

Thembi's blog was often moving and, because she had a wonderful sense of humor, sometimes funny as well. She wrote, for example, that she was excited about staying at a "mansion" that foreign tourists visited in her country. She expected great luxury, but she found "the beer, the food, the music, the low light was exactly like places in Khayelitsha ... The difference here was that these were all white people sitting on the floor with no shoes on. In Khayelitsha we sit on chairs, wear shoes, and there are no white people. I thought, my god, these people are imitating the township life! I want to be rich and these rich people are pretending to be poor."

The year Thembi toured South Africa, UNICEF also sponsored her travel to Germany, to a meeting of world leaders, and to India. She didn't like the conference in Germany

From Thembi's
South African Blog:
March 7–8, 2007
We woke at 3:45 a.m. for our morning flight ... We were tiiired! In one blink I was suddenly at the U.S. Consulate and the Consul General was bombarding me with questions. He was a nice man and complimented me on my courage. It still surprises me why everyone thinks this is so courageous when I feel I am just being me.

much, because of "sitting down all day in fancy rooms with people standing in front of projectors … and using these big words." In India, she met many wonderful women who, like herself, were working to convince people to speak out about having AIDS. She said she learned from these women that "you don't need money to do certain things. If you have your hands, you have your mouth, you have your brain, then you can just speak." In 2008, Thembi also went to Mexico City to speak at the International AIDS Conference.

Wherever she went, media interviewed her. They wanted to know more about this small woman – Thembi was less than five feet (1.5 m) tall – who had such a big personality and influence. Often, they would ask about her daughter. Thembi said having Onwabo meant, "I love my life now." And even when considering the possibility that she may not live to see her daughter grow up, she spoke positively: "whether I'm here or not, I know she's going to be part of me. Everything is going to be fine." Onwabo was just under four years old at the time of this interview in 2008. Thembi also said, of course, she wished she didn't have the illness, "but I'm happy."

In April 2009, Thembi celebrated her twenty-fourth birthday. Her family received some incredible news about this time. Melikhaya had been tested again for HIV, and the result was negative! The original test had been incorrect; he didn't have the virus.

It had now been eight years since Thembi had been diagnosed, and she had had only one instance of life-threatening sickness. Still, when she was recording a visit to her doctor for the diary, he told her AIDS was "very much like swimming in a lake where you have crocodiles. You can swim for some time without getting bit, but if you stay for a long time, at some point you are going to get bitten." There are many risks to the illness; one is that the body becomes so weak from the virus, it can't fight off other infections. That is what happened to Thembi. She got a form of tuberculosis, and in June 2009, she died.

Thembi always knew her AIDS could be fatal. Although she said she had to think of her own death and dying every day, she didn't dwell on it. She focused on life, saying, "You must do something while you're still alive." What she did touched so many that after her death she was paid tribute in Africa, across North America, and in Britain. Joe Richman said Thembi was the "most alive" person he ever met, and that she had given him, and many others, "a lesson in courage and in embracing the craziness of life." When radio listeners heard the news, they posted their thoughts on NPR's website, the network where her diary originally aired. One listener wrote of her "awesome sense of dignity." Another thanked her for her devotion to truth. Still another wrote, "Oh, that voice of hers."

When she was interviewed about the diary in 2006, Thembi told the reporter, with her usual lovely sense of humor, "I always wanted to be a journalist, even when I was growing up, because I know that I talk too much." Thembi did not talk too much. She chose to tell a story in order to help others. Through her bravery, vibrant spirit, and of course, her wonderful voice, Thembi and that story live on.

Thembi Ngubane – a lesson in courage

GLOSSARY

Assignment: the stories journalists work on are sometimes called assignments. Someone at their place of work will assign them to report on a particular story.

Behind the scenes: there are many more journalists involved in putting out newspaper, television, radio, magazine, and Internet reports than the ones whose names are on a story or who you see or hear. Researchers, editors, and producers are some examples of people who work "behind the scenes." It is called "behind the scenes" because the public doesn't see it.

Cover a story: a journalist who covers a story is "on" that story; she or he is assigned to gather information about that story.

Journalist: anyone involved in gathering and putting together truthful information for factual stories, particularly stories of public value and interest.

Reporter: a person who goes out and gathers news and information, and is usually the one who is the public face on the story. This is the person you see reporting on TV, hear on the radio, or whose name is under the headline in a print story. Reporters are journalists. But not all journalists are reporters: some work behind the scenes in other kinds of journalism jobs (*see above*).

SOURCES
AND RESOURCES

Mary Ann Shadd Cary

Bearden, Jim and Linda Jean Butler. *Shadd; The Life and Times of Mary Shadd Cary.* Toronto: NC Press Ltd., 1977.

Finkelman, Paul (editor). *Encyclopedia of the United States in the Nineteenth Century.* Edition 1. Charles Scribner's Sons, 2000.

Rhodes, Jane. *Mary Ann Shadd Cary; The Black Press and Protest in the Nineteenth Century.* Bloomington, IN: Indiana University Press, 1998.

Smith, Tom W. "Changing Racial Labels; From 'Colored' to 'Negro' to 'Black' to 'African-American.'" *Public Opinion Quarterly*, Volume 56, 1992.

Streitmatter, Rodger. *Raising her Voice: African-American Women Journalists who Changed History.* University Press of Kentucky, 1994.

Nellie Bly

Kroeger, Brooke. *Nellie Bly: Daredevil, Reporter, Feminist.* Random House, 1994.

"Nellie Bly, Journalist, Dies of Pneumonia." *The New York Times.* January 28, 1922. Available from: http://www.nytimes.com

Public Broadcasting Service (PBS). *Around the World in 72 Days.* Broadcast on *The American Experience,* a production of WGBH/ Boston, 1997.
The website for this PBS program has many useful resources. http://www.pbs.org/wgbh/amex/world/

Singer, Ben. *Melodrama and Modernity. Early Sensational Cinema and its Contexts.* New York: Columbia University Press, 2001.

The website of the National Women's Hall of Fame, in Seneca Falls, New York, has good biographies of many notable women, including Nellie Bly.
http://www.greatwomen.org/

Margaret Bourke-White
Bourke-White, Margaret. *Dear Fatherland, Rest Quietly.* Simon and Schuster, 1946.

Bourke-White, Margaret. *Portrait of Myself.* Simon and Schuster, 1963.

Bourke-White, Margaret and Erskine Caldwell. *You Have Seen Their Faces.* New York: Modern Age Books, Inc., 1937.

Bourke-White, Margaret and Sean Callahan (Contributor). *Margaret-Bourke White: Photographer.* Little, Brown and Co., 1998.

Goldberg, Vicki. *Margaret Bourke-White, A Biography.* New York: Harper & Row Publishers, 1986.

"The Great Achiever." *Time Magazine.* September 6, 1971.

Doris Anderson
Anderson, Doris. *Rebel Daughter; An Autobiography.* Toronto: Key Porter Books, 1996.

Burke, Jasmyn. "The Anderson Mystique." *Ryerson Review of Journalism*, Special Anniversary Issue. Summer 2008.

CBC Television, *Life and Times* documentary series. *The Life and Times of Doris Anderson*. February 26, 1997.

Korinek, Valerie J. *Roughing It in the Suburbs: Reading Chatelaine Magazine in the Fifties and Sixties*. Toronto: University of Toronto Press, 2000.

Library and Archives Canada website. "Celebrating Women's Achievements; Doris Anderson." http://www.collectionscanada.gc.ca/femmes/002026-295-e.html

Martin, Sandra. "Doris Anderson, Journalist and Political Activist." *The Globe and Mail*. March 3, 2007.

Barbara Frum

"Barbara Frum: 1937-1992 'Leading Broadcaster of her generation' Journal host was undeterred by leukemia." *Toronto Star*. March 26, 1992.

CBC Television, *Life and Times* documentary series. *The Life and Times of Barbara Frum*. September 17, 2002.

Corelli, Rae. "A Death in the Family." *Maclean's*. April 6, 1992.

Frum, Linda. *Barbara Frum, A Daughter's Memoir*. Toronto: Random House of Canada, 1996.

Knelman, Martin. "*Journal* marked high point for CBC." *Toronto Star*. January 10, 2007.

Mitchell, Alanna with CP. "Barbara Frum Journalistic icon had her feet firmly on the ground." *The Globe and Mail*. March 27, 1992.

Useful website providing biographies of Barbara Frum and others: Heroines.ca A Guide to Women in Canadian History http://www.heroines.ca/

Katie Couric

Auletta, Ken. "The Dawn Patrol." *The New Yorker.* August 8, 2005.

Carter, Bill. "Walters, Canny Survivor, Adds It All Up." *The New York Times.* May 5, 2008.

Donlon, Brian. "Couric the catalyst." *USA Today.* April 14,1992.

Franklin, Nancy. "Katie Couric's ill-fated voyage with CBS." *The New Yorker.* May 26, 2008.

Koestler-Grack, Rachel A. *Katie Couric: Groundbreaking TV Journalist.* Pleasantville, NY: Gareth Stevens, 2009.

Mackey, Maureen. "Katie Couric faces the toughest challenge of her career." *Reader's Digest.* February 2007. Available from: *Reader'sDigest.com*

Roberts, Roxanne. "Yipes! It's Katie Couric!" *The Washington Post.* May 21, 1991.

Schwarzbaum, Lisa. "Katie Couric Did It." *Entertainment* Weekly. July 31, 1992.

Shales,Tom. "Katie Couric, at Home with Bush." *The Washington Post.* October 14, 1992.

Stelter, Brian. "Doubts Fade and Couric is Energized." *The New York Times.* September 20, 2009.

Traister, Rebecca. "The Cruella Syndrome." *Salon.com.* March 18, 2004.

Wyatt, Edward. "Coming Back to Hard News; Katherine Anne Couric." *The New York Times.* April 6, 2006.

Williams, Lena. "The Woman Who Replaced Jane Pauley's Replacement." *The New York Times.* April 8, 1991.

Zakaria, Fareed. "Palin is Ready? Please." *Newsweek*. October 6, 2008.

Anna Politkovskaya
Bergkraut, Eric (Director). *Letter to Anna*. Documentary film, 2008.

Gould, Terry. *Murder without Borders – Dying for the Story in the World's Most Dangerous Places.*
Toronto: Random House Canada, 2009.

Knight, Amy. "Who Killed Anna Politkovskaya?" *The New York Review of Books*. November 6, 2008.

Meek, James. "The Best Memorial." *The Guardian*. October 14, 2006.

Meek, James. "Dispatches from a Savage War." *The Guardian*. October 15, 2004.

Politkovskaya, Anna. *Putin's Russia: Life in a Failing Democracy*. Metropolitan Books, 2005.

Politkovskaya, Anna. Speech on receiving *IWMF Courage in Journalism Award* from International Women's Media Foundation. October 2002.

Skaggs, Cal (Producer and Director). *Democracy on Deadline: the Global Struggle for an Independent Press*. PBS Documentary. November 21, 2006.

Specter, Michael. "Kremlin, Inc. Why are Vladimir Putin's opponents dying?" *The New Yorker*. January 29, 2007.

Useful website for information about Russia and Chechnya:
BBC News http://news.bbc.co.uk/

Useful websites for information about Journalists and Freedom:
Committee to Protect Journalists www.cpj.org/
Reporters Without Borders www.rsf.org/

Pam Oliver

Chambers, Deborah, Linda Steiner and Carole Fleming. *Women and Journalism*. New York: Routledge, 2004.

Crysdale, Joy. Interview with Pam Oliver. December 2009.

Fleischman, Bill. "Fox's Oliver gets kudos for sideline reporting." *Philadelphia Daily News*. January 16, 2004.

Gite Lloyd. "Pam Oliver." *Essence*. September 1996.

Hoffman, Melody K. "Going beyond the X's and O's." *Jet*. May 26, 2008.

Oliver, B.L. "Fox Sports is prepared to put on a Super show." *New York Amsterdam News*. February 3, 2005.

"Pam Oliver." *Current Biography Monthly Magazine*. H.W.Wilson, database publisher. July 2009.

Schultz, Brad. *Sports Media – Reporting, Producing and Planning*. Elsevier, 2005.

Silver, Mike and Brett Martin. "73 Reasons We're Living in a New Golden Age of Football." *GQ Gentlemen's Quarterly*. September, 2008.

Suggs, Ernie. "Fox Sports broadcaster and A&M alum Pam Oliver garners much respect in a man's world." *Knight Ridder/Tribune*. August 18, 2002.

Farida Nekzad

Armstrong, Sally. *Bitter Roots, Tender Shoots – the Uncertain Fate of Afghanistan's Women*. Toronto: Viking Canada, 2008.

Crysdale, Joy. Interview with Farida Nekzad, by email. November 2009.

Gangat, Sharmeen. "Nekzad Defies Warlords to Tell Women's Stories." *Womensenews.org*. December 5, 2008.

Interview with Farida Nekzad. Government of Canada website, July 21, 2008.
afghanistan.gc.ca/Canada-afghanistan/

Simpson, Peggy. "Afghan Journalist Speaks Out for Women, Press Freedom." International Women's Media Foundation. October 8, 2008. Available from:
http://www.iwmf.org/article.aspx?id=750&c=carticles

Useful Websites about Women in News Media, and Afghanistan:
International Women's Media Foundation iwmf.org
Voices on the Rise voicesontherise.org

Thembi Ngubane
Crysdale, Joy. Interview with Joe Richman. November 2009.

Nelson, Erika. "First Person – Thembi Ngubane." *The Body – The Complete HIV/AIDS Resource*. August 3, 2008.

Ngubane, Thembi "Thembi's AIDS Diary Tour: South Africa." Various dates, 2007.
Blog: http://thembisaidsdiarytour.vox.com/

Ngubane, Thembi and Joe Richman (producer). "Thembi's AIDS Diary – A Year in the Life of a South African Teenager." *National Public Radio*. April 2006.

Pressley Montes, Sue Anne. "Living in the face of AIDS." *Telegraph-Journal*, Saint John, New Brunswick. April 29, 2006.

UNAIDS/WHO/UNICEF Epidemiological fact sheets on HIV and AIDS, 2008. http://www.unaids.org/en/KnowledgeCentre/HIVData/Epidemiology/epifactsheets.asp

ACKNOWLEDGMENTS

This book was publisher Margie Wolfe's idea, and I can't thank her enough for giving me the opportunity to do it. Editor Debbie Rogosin was a gift. She was encouraging and generous in her feedback, and her thoughtful input made this a much better book. I'm so grateful to her. Thank you to everyone at Second Story Press – you are an amazing group. My dear friend Karen Levine helped pull me out of the mire more than once. Another dear friend, Anne McNeilly, contributed her talented and expert eyes.

Many wonderful journalist friends cheered me on, and I was, and am, so appreciative. They also made great suggestions of women who could be featured in the book; I wish I could have included all of them, as well as those fearless female journalists in my own circle. Geraldine Sherman and Bob Fulford were incredibly helpful with the Barbara Frum chapter, remembering their cherished friend.

Librarians are some of the world's best people, I've decided. So to my Humber colleagues, Mark Bryant and Denise Rooney, and to those anonymous librarians at Toronto Public Library, thank you for your patience and guidance. I couldn't have done the chapter on Afghanistan without the assistance of Julie

Payne with Canadian Journalists for Free Expression, or the full story of Thembi Ngubane without producer Joe Richman. Thank you. Mike Strizic made excellent notes on some challenging Couric material, and I am grateful to him, and student Kelly Roche, who suggested Pam Oliver. The Ontario Arts Council has my great appreciation as well for its work supporting writers, including me. And finally, many thanks to the dean and my associate dean at the School of Media Studies at Humber, William Hanna and Basil Guinane, for their support and for providing me the opportunity to work with students, teaching the craft and profession I so dearly love.

Joy Crysdale

PHOTO CREDITS

page 52: Courtesy Jeff Wyonch

page 55: Courtesy Michael Rickard

page 61: Courtesy Steve Rogers

page 65: © GetStock, artist: jeremy sutton-hibbert, collection: Almay

page 73: Courtesy Evgeniya Zubchenko

page 75: © FOX Sports

page 80: © FOX Sports/Pam Oliver

page 85: Courtesy iwmfphotos/Flickr Creative Commons

page 87: © Steve Evans

page 90: © Leslie Knott

page 95: © Melikhaya Mpumela

page 101: © Melikhaya Mpumela

page 104: © Melikhaya Mpumela

The Women's Hall of Fame Series

Nobel's Women of PEACE

Michelle Benjamin and Maggie Rooney

The Women's Hall of Fame Series

Fantastic Female Filmmakers

Suzanne Simoni

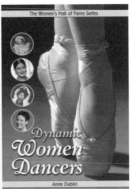

The Women's Hall of Fame Series

Dynamic Women Dancers

Anne Dublin

More from The Women's Hall of Fame Series

The Women's Hall of Fame Series

ASTONISHING WOMEN ARTISTS

Heather Ball

The Women's Hall of Fame Series

Incredible Women Inventors

Sandra Braun

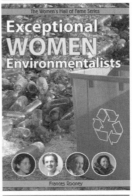

The Women's Hall of Fame Series

Exceptional WOMEN Environmentalists

Frances Rooney

The Women's Hall of Fame Series

EXTRAORDINARY WOMEN EXPLORERS

FRANCES ROONEY

The Women's Hall of Fame Series

SPECTACULAR WOMEN IN SPACE

Sonia Gueldenpfennig

The Women's Hall of Fame Series

MAGNIFICENT WOMEN IN MUSIC

Heather Ball

The Women's Hall of Fame Series

Remarkable Women Writers

Heather Ball

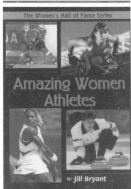

The Women's Hall of Fame Series

Amazing Women Athletes

by Jill Bryant

The Women's Hall of Fame Series

GREAT WOMEN LEADERS

HEATHER BALL

The Women's Hall of Fame Series

Fabulous Female Physicians

by Sharon Kirsh with Florence Kirsh

The Women's Hall of Fame Series

SUPER WOMEN IN SCIENCE

by Kelly Di Domenico